RISK, PORTFOLIO MANAGEMENT AND CAPITAL MARKETS

Risk, Portfolio Management and Capital Markets

Edited by

T. E. Cooke
Department of Economics
University of Exeter

J. Matatko
Department of Economics
University of Exeter

and

D. C. Stafford
sometime Head of the Department of Economics
University of Exeter

M
MACMILLAN

First published 1992

Published by
MACMILLAN ACADEMIC AND PROFESSIONAL LTD
Houndmills, Basingstoke, Hampshire RG21 2XS
and London
Companies and representatives
throughout the world

Printed in Hong Kong

British Library Cataloguing in Publication Data
Risk, portfolio management and capital markets.
1. Investment
I. Cooke, Terence E. *1952–* II. Matatko, John *1946–*
III. Stafford, D. C. (David Christopher) *1943–89*
332.6
ISBN 0–333·52605–8

This volume is dedicated to the memory of David Stafford, whose tragic and untimely death occurred while the volume was in preparation.

Contents

List of Figures

List of Tables

Notes on the Contributors

Alan Bainbridge is a consultant with KPMG. He holds degrees from the University of Cambridge and the London Business School and is a Fellow of the Institute of Chartered Accountants in England and Wales. He also won a three-month exchange scholarship to Chicago Business School to study finance. Much of his audit experience was gained in the financial services area, particularly merchant banks, discount houses and commodity brokers. As well as his audit experience he has also been involved in advising clients on information system requirements and activity-based costing systems.

David Blake is Lecturer in Financial Economics at Birkbeck College, University of London. He was formerly Director of the Securities Industry Programme at City University Business School and Research Fellow at the London Business School and the London School of Economics. He is consultant to many organisations, including James Capel, the Independent Television Companies Association, J. Henry Schroder Wagg, the Bankers Trust and UNESCO. His research interests include the modelling of asset demands, the investment behaviour and performance of UK pensions funds, financial innovations, and macroeconometrics. He has published in major economics and finance journals in all these fields, and is the author of Financial Market Analysis, published in 1990.

T. E. Cooke is a Reader in Accountancy at the University of Exeter and is holder of an ICAEW Fellowship. His research interests are in mergers and acquisitions and corporate financial reporting. He has had articles accepted for publication in *Accounting and Business Research*, *Accounting, Business and Financial History*, *British Accounting Review*, *International Journal of Accounting*, *Journal of Accounting and Public Policy*, *Journal of Business Finance and Accounting* and *Journal of International Financial Management and Accounting*. He is author of *Mergers and Acquisitions* (1986), *International Mergers and Acquisitions* (1988), *European Financial Reporting: Sweden* (1988), and *Empirical Study of Financial Disclosure by Swedish Companies* (1989) and co-author of *Financial and Treasury Management* (1988) and *Financial Reporting in Japan: Regulation, Practice and Environment* (forthcoming).

Desmond Corner was formerly Reader in Finance and Director of MA in Finance and Investment, University of Exeter. He is Director of Dartmoor Investment Trust PLC and Exeter Fund Managers. He is co-author of *Investment Trusts in Britain and America, Open-end Funds in the EEC and Switzerland*, co-editor of *Modern Portfolio Theory and Financial Institutions*, and author of articles on finance in several academic journals.

David Damant is the Managing Director of Paribas Asset Management (UK), the UK investment management division with Banque Paribas, which is the 28th largest bank in the world. He has a degree in logic and scientific method from the University of Cambridge, where he was an analyst and fund manager, and where he developed methodologies for technical analysis and for modern portfolio theory, offering a service for index matching the London equity market in 1977. He was subsequently a partner in stockbrokers Quilter Goodison & Company (Executive Committee) and is a member of the International Stock Exchange. He is a former Chairman and currently a Fellow of the Society of Investment Analysts in the United Kingdom. He is a former President of the European Federation of Financial Analysts Societies and now represents the European Federation on the International Coordinating Committee of Financial Analysts Associations worldwide. He represents that committee on the Board of the International Accounting Standards Committee, which is the body which establishes accounting standards on the world level. Mr Damant was a member of the former Accounting Standards Committee in the United Kingdom and is secretary of the Institute of Quantitative Investment Research.

Robert G. Luther is a Lecturer in Exeter University's Department of Economics. He spent four years with Deloitte, Haskins & Sells in South Africa, where he trained as a chartered accountant. He is also a management accountant and was, until recently, with Peat Marwick McLintock. His research interests include profit-sharing schemes, the financing of mining companies and ethical investments.

John Matatko is Director of the graduate programme in finance and investment at Exeter University. He is co-author of *Key Developments in Personal Finance* and co-editor of the *Directory of Unit Trust Management*, as well as publishing a range of papers in the finance area. He has also acted as consultant to numerous private and public bodies, such as the Consumers' Association and the Unit Trust Association, and is currently directing an industry-funded project on financial intermediation.

Charles Owen-Conway is by training a corporate lending banker and has held posts in a variety of branches and Head Office departments of National Westminster Bank. He is presently part of a team involved in the development and marketing of capital markets products with a particular emphasis on interest-rate risk management.

Andrew Perrins studied mathematics at Southampton University before training as an actuary, qualifying in 1987. In August 1990 he was responsible for the launch of the 'Protected Growth Investment', the only UK authorised unit trust allowing investors to participate in equity market growth whilst protecting them against price falls over *any* one year period. Earlier in 1990 he presented a paper on capital protection to the International Actuarial Association in Paris. He works as a fund manager at Abbey Life, where he is responsible for asset allocation and quantitative products.

Jane Platt is a Director of BZW Investment Management. During the past ten years she has managed investments in a wide variety of markets, moving from an active to a quantitative approach. She is therefore one of the few UK investment professionals to have experience of both traditional and technology-based fund management.

Richard Purkis is Lecturer in Finance at Exeter University. He read economics at Exeter University, is a chartered accountant and has an MBA from the Cranfield School of Management. He was co-editor (with D. Stafford) of the *Macmillan Directory of Multinationals 1989*. He was a compiling editor of the *International Stock Exchange Yearbook*, 1989-90 edition.

Richard Stevens is a partner in the Capital Markets Group of Price Waterhouse in London. He graduated from the University of Bristol with a degree in economics and accounting and qualified as a chartered accountant with Price Waterhouse. Shortly after qualifying as a chartered accountant he became the Assistant to the Chairman of the Accounting Standards Committee. Richard was a member of UK Auditing Practices Committee Sub-Committee responsible for the audit guideline for banking audits. His experience with Price Waterhouse embraces accounting practices employed by banking institutions in the United Kingdom, United States, Europe and the Middle East. As an audit partner in the Price Waterhouse Capital Markets Group he is responsible for the audit of a number of significant financial institutions involved in the development of, and trading in, capital markets instruments.

David Stafford was sometime Head of the Department of Economics at the University of Exeter. He was co-author of *Open-end Funds in the EEC and Switzerland* and of *Key Developments* in *Personal Finance* and co-editor of the *Directory of Unit Trust Management*. He published articles widely in the fields of housing economics and finance.

Toru Takenashi is a fund manager with Nomura Securities Investment Trust Managemet Co. Ltd. in Tokyo. He graduated from the Tokyo University of Technology and joined Nomura Securities, working in the Tokyo Research Department. He has held positions in both investment management systems and planning. He graduated from the MA in finance and investment at the University of Exeter in 1989.

Acknowledgements

The editors, and conference organisers, wish to acknowledge with great appreciation the generous support of the following institutions in the promotion of the conference held at the University of Exeter in September 1989, in which this book is based:

Barclays Bank plc
Lloyds Abbey Life
National Westminster Bank plc
Peat Marwick McLintock

The editors and publishers also wish to thank the following for permission to reproduce copyright material:

Abbey Life, for Figures 2.1–2.3.
BZW, for Figures 3.1–3.9.
NatWest, for figures 6.1 and 6.2.
Bank of England Quarterly Bulletin (November 1988), for data in Table 5.2.
Nomura IT, for data in Table 8.11, from *A Handbook of Investment Trusts* (1987).
Morgan Stanley (1987) for Table 8.13.

Introduction

Since the worldwide stock market crash of 1987, the word 'risk' has assumed a vital significance in practical investment terminology. While it is true that for almost 25 years academic work on capital markets has been two-dimensional, return *and* risk, many investment practitioners considered the rigorous, quantitative view of the second dimension as arcane and unnecessary. All that was necessary in this view was the selection of 'good' or 'under-valued' securities. With the sudden and dramatic fall in stock markets in October 1987 came the realisation that the 'risk' to which a portfolio was exposed needed to be analysed and, if possible, quantified. If such analysis could be successfully applied, then although the risk dimension could not be eliminated it could be controlled or even set at a pre-selected level. The client of the investment manager could be offered a product where, although the possibility of loss could not be eliminated, at least it was clearly labelled. This volume reports the papers presented to a meeting of financial 'practitioners', sprinkled with academics, each study dealing with an aspect of the process of understanding and managing 'risky' assets. The volume is in three parts: The Revolution in Equity Management; 'Special Problems'; 'Developments in Accounting and Finance'.

The tone of Part I is set by Chapter 1, 'The Revolution in Investment Management', the paper presented by David Damant of Paribas Asset Management. Damant's argument stems from the recognition that the principal factor of control in managing a portfolio is asset allocation. Stock selection, except in achieving clearly defined portfolio tilts, is seen as relatively unrewarding. It is the asset mix: cash/equities/bonds/currency, etc., which is the primary vehicle for portfolio control. Indeed as world stock markets become more information 'efficient', index funds become the vehicle for both domestic and international equity investment. Damant's arguments are illustrated and applied in two separate approaches by the following two papers. Chapter 2, 'An Introduction to Capital Protection Strategies', by Andrew Perrins of Abbey Life IS, spells out for the investor various approaches to achieving a 'floor' level of return (i.e., an amount below which a client portfolio cannot fall) while still permitting participation in stock market rises ('upside-capture'). More than one method is available to achieve this result and Perrins makes clear the costs and benefits of, and the judgements needed in, each of these attempts to control and limit investor risk exposure. The approach to portfolio management in Chapter 3, 'Asset Allocation: a Case Study' by Jane Platt of Barclays de Zoete Wedd, is somewhat more classical. Her case study of institutional fund management uses the mean–variance portfolio choice framework to establish a 'minimum risk' international portfolio of bonds and equities. However, what her study makes particularly plain is the need of the fund manager for a whole battery of techniques. Quantitative methods, for example, are used in establishing the 'risk' inputs to the programming process, since much previous work indicates that these estimates are statistically reliable. However, judgement plays its part both in the forecasting of expected returns and in 'fine-tuning' the portfolio to the needs of the particular client. Lastly David Blake, of Birkbeck College, presents in Chapter 4 a formal model of portfolio choice when the means, variances and covariances of a portfolio selection problem vary systematically over time.

In Part II special problems of various aspects of the capital markets are explored. The gilts market, investment trusts, new Japanese index futures contracts and interest rate swaps separately form the bases of the four papers. Chapter 5, 'Tax Effects in Gilt-Edged Security Valuation', by Robert Luther and John Matatko of the University of Exeter, attempts to solve a fundamental problem in asset valuation. Included in the valuation of government bonds are necessarily a set of interest rates. The deduction of what these market rates of interest actually are is of primary importance in valuation of these and other assets. However, the prices of government bonds are also affected by the non-uniform tax treatment of those holding them. The paper estimates both the overall 'effective' tax rates in the gilt-edged market, and simultaneously estimates the term structure of interest rates. Also concerned with interest rates from a different point of view is Chapter 6, 'Interest Rate Management', by Charles Owen-Conway of National Westminster Bank. The detailed coverage in this paper of techniques for active interest rate management provides a clear 'menu' for corporate finance directors seeking to control their debt financing costs.

The question of the use of investment trust discounts in decision making is examined empirically by John Matatko and Richard Purkis of Exeter University in Chapter 7, 'Investment Trust Price Discounts'. Investment trust discounts fluctuate over time for reasons which are not yet well explained. If we accept this ignorance, can these fluctuations still be used to generate profits? Some US studies indicate that such is indeed the case. Using the comprehensive Association of Investment Trust Companies Database, the authors attempt to answer this question for the UK. Finally Chapter 8, 'New Japanese Index Futures Contracts', by Desmond Corner and Toru Takenashi of Exeter University and Nomura Asset Management, respectively, describes the features of the new Japanese futures contracts offered in Tokyo on the Nikkei-Dow and Topix indices. The importance of the work can be judged from the fact that previously the only such futures contracts available were the Nikkei not in Tokyo but on SIMEX, and a restricted index available in Osaka. Previous work has shown the somewhat anomalous behaviour of the prices of the older contracts, the new contracts therefore add a new possibility of risk control on the Tokyo market.

Part III links finance with accounting. Alan Bainbridge's Chapter 9, 'Problems of Assessing Risk and Return Inside an Operating Business', outlines approaches to the assessment of risk and return on physical assets within operating businesses. Whilst the contents of the paper do not provide any new approaches it serves to highlight the need for a carefully considered programme of physical investment appraisal. The paper considers the estimation of the cost of capital using the capital–asset pricing model (CAPM) and assumes that the risk of the market portfolio and the risk (beta) of individual securities can be obtained using historical data. Having discussed the relationship between risk and return the paper discusses how a project's risk can be estimated by relating the operating leverage and revenue sensitivity of the project to other assets. Assuming that a risk-free rate can be established, these assumptions permit the use of a single discount rate to evaluate the cash flows in different periods for a capital investment project.

Richard Steven's Chapter 10, 'Problems of Income Recognition in a Capital Markets Institution', deals with emerging issues in accounting for new financial instruments. Problems surround recognition at reporting dates during the life of a transaction; some have argued that such financial instruments should be accounted for using a 'marking to market' approach, the practice of recording an instrument at its market price at an interim reporting date. Whilst this approach has been advocated to deal with problems of income recognition in a capital markets institution, in practice marking to market is not easy and regulatory responses have been slow. Whilst departures from historical cost accounting have been legally permissible for some time – for example, it has been legal to revalue property and investments held as trading portfolio since 1948 – the most widespread departure as far as financial services companies are concerned relates to the valuation of swaps, options, futures and other relevant financial services products. The need to resolve the accounting issues of such transactions stems from the requirement to present the results of the underlying economic activity at an interim reporting date.

The practical difficulties of marking to market include the situation where a market does not exist or where the market is thin, and whether the bid, mid-market or other rates should be used and in what circumstances. In practice, other companies use a hotchpotch of historical cost and market value accounting which has brought about ranges in values that do not adequately reflect the economic performance for the period. The regulatory response to the challenges of accounting for new financial instruments has been extremely slow. The Accounting Standards Committee has now begun to address such issues, and the EC Fourth Directive on Company Accounts applies to non-bank financial institutions but does not address the key issues. However, the Financial Accounting Standards Board in the US has a project which is expected to develop broad srandards aimed at resolving key issues and providing for more consistent practice.

T.E. Cooke

J. Matatko

Part I
The Revolution in Equity Management

1 The Revolution in Investment Management

David Damant

We are in the presence of very definite revolution in investment analysis and portfolio construction, the seeds of which were planted in the last, say, twenty five years. A 'revolution' is a very dramatic change, a change in the theoretical background, and in the practical methodologies. This is not everywhere apparent but it will shortly be so – within, say, five to seven years. Things are already different, and after that lapse of time they will be completely different. The change in the way in which the subject is viewed will be as different as the way in which the structure of societies was viewed after the French Revolution, as compared with the *ancien régime*.

A starting place in this analysis is the rise of the so-called Modern Portfolio Theory (MPT), the Efficient Market Theory, the Capital Asset Pricing Model, and so on. Of course, trends in this direction are fundamental to the thesis that we have seen a revolution; but they are not the whole story, because the arrival of new technology and the internationalisation of our business (and these two last points are of course connected) would have created a very considerable revolution quite apart from the rise of MPT as such. But MPT is a useful way into the topic. I will discuss the whole question in the context of equity investment, although many elements in the argument apply also to bonds.

Many of the elements of MPT originated as a result of the invention of the computer and its application to the investment business. Statisticians had for a long time been interested in streams of data (such as rainfall figures) and when computers gave them the power to analyse more series more quickly they turned their attention to the stock exchange. They found, as you will be aware, that share prices moved substantially in a random walk and this, I understand, is a result which the statisticians did not wholly expect. And, when they looked for a model of how such a stream of random prices might be generated, they came up with the Efficient Market Hypothesis: Paul

Samuelson and others demonstrated that if prices were properly anticipated, a random series would be the result.

The concept that markets are efficient in the sense that future prospects for shares and economies are correctly discounted requires also the concept of risk, because the discount factor which must be applied to future earnings or dividends to arrive at a present value will vary according to the risks run – that is, according to the uncertainties which may govern the future prospects for a company as opposed to a government bond. One of the main contributions of MPT to our business is that the idea of risk is fully integrated into the picture. When Markowitz wrote his seminal paper, and Sharpe simplified it into the Capital Asset Pricing Model (CAPM), the clear trade-off in efficient markets between return and risk was formalised as central to the whole investment problem.

One way of looking at the characteristics of an efficient market is to say that the market is by definition cleverer than you are, and therefore there is nothing much that you can do about the investment problem except to watch and follow what other investors, in their collective wisdom, are doing. This approach is sometimes called 'technical', as opposed to 'fundamental' which is the adjective applied to the basics of a company or economy. 'Technical' is of course the approach traditionally adopted by the chartists, or technical analysts. One of the surprising things in the development of MPT is that the people who have developed the various methods of MPT, based upon an efficient market, do not see the chartists as essentially allies, the forerunners of the more scientific approach. This argument has met with no great enthusiasm either from the efficient market people or from chartists. As Aneurin Bevan said, 'Those who walk in the middle of the road usually get run over': but this is a subject in itself. Incidentally, the newspaper report that a Bank of England study had come to the conclusion that chartists operating in the currency markets came up with results no better than random was misleading: the full report is more supportive of the use of charts.

We had, then, a situation – say, by the end of the 1960s – in which a thorough-going theory had been formulated concerning the stock exchange, and a formidable amount of scientific evidence had been produced by academics to support it. Note that, previously, the stock exchange had been a very peculiar phenomenon, with no one really knowing why it did what it did. One would have therefore thought that the new approach would have been embraced both by outsiders to the profession – who could see, for the first time, that something rational was going on – and by insiders, who might like to formulate new techniques and achieve a better control over the investment problem.

Not at all. Outsiders still – even in the US where these theories are much more widely known than elsewhere – seem to know very little, and to disbelieve what they do know about the Efficient Market Theory. A very important example is company management. Company directors frequently believe that their shares are undervalued on the market, that their brand names are not properly appreciated, and that the market is moved by large tides of fashion which bear no resemblance to economic or commercial reality. It is difficult, and indeed impossible, to persuade company management of the validity of the efficient market approach: directors attending well organised seminars stare in disbelief when the possibility that the market may be taking rational views is emphasised by very well qualified speakers. This is a very serious matter: directors may take decisions in the real economy based upon a false appreciation of the capital markets, with real, and undesirable, effects. There are also consequences for accounting theory – if the market is efficient an accounting change which merely moves the numbers in the annual report around the page cannot make any difference to a share price valuation: the directors generally believe that it does. Much of the controversies about accounting for brands, or goodwill, stem from this belief. If the facts about MPT could be more widely accepted outside the investment business, another revolution would take place which would be of very large benefit to society, and especially to the efficient use of capital.

Insiders, as was perhaps to be expected, also reacted negatively to the ideas of MPT. It was for a long time quite a joke in the United States that every university which had studied the question had come to the conclusion that markets (at least the major share markets in the US) were efficient, whereas not a single university endowment fund had taken any notice of this conclusion. Obviously, investment professionals felt threatened but after the bear market of 1973–74 and perhaps because after such a fall people thought that there must be a better way – the new ideas began to catch on in the States. First, with index funds; and obviously if the market is very efficient a passive buy and hold strategy of a properly diversified list of shares is the only reasonable conclusion. But even so the build up was slow and there was a lot of opposition to the idea. Attempts to sell the ideas in London in the late 1970s fell on deaf ears, even though there is always a very large amount of traffic between London and New York. Why ideas should take time to travel I do not know. It is a question which is perhaps outside the scope of this seminar, and it applies to all types of things, including card games and other fashions as well as investment theory. But as you will be aware the tide reached the UK only around 1984–85, except for a few special exceptions, and has reached significant levels only after another crash, that of 1987.

One of the reasons why there was so much resistance to the idea of MPT might have been that the academics in question were very hardline. I have heard it said that at the University of Chicago that it was impossible to get a Ph.D at one time if you claimed that there were inefficiencies in the market. In the middle 1970s I myself heard the Efficient Market Theory compared to the second law of thermodynamics: a mistake of enormous importance since it showed no understanding on the part of the speaker (a professor who was in favour of the efficiency of markets) that theories concerning a human phenomenon like the stock exchange can hardly be compared with very general physical laws which admit, as far as we can see at the moment, of no exceptions. But gradually, of course, not only did the ideas of MPT become more accepted, but also the academics changed their tune and most universities and indeed commercial organisations involved in quantitative research are now looking for inefficiencies. The fact that a market contains numerous inefficiencies, allowing money to be made, does not of course mean that the market is seriously inefficient. The pricing of shares is still, usually, very close to reality.

The actual products which result from these trends will be reasonably familiar. The first move is very often with index funds although even before this type of passive investment becomes accepted some type of risk analysis may win a degree of acceptance, perhaps because producing a risk profile of a traditionally managed portfolio is regarded as a useful 'add on', not threatening the traditional techniques themselves. On the whole, however, the arrival of the index fund concept indicates that quantitative ideas have arrived. And the appeal of index funds is chiefly seen in markets which have a high degree of efficiency: an index fund might be a useful way of investing in a small inefficient market if the investor in question wishes to limit his risks and in any case has not the resources to devote to digging out inefficiencies; but chiefly it is in the large well organised markets that index funds will grow and the percentage achieved – even already in the US – may be surprisingly high.

Index funds are often identified with passive management but in fact other types of passive portfolio are possible. These may often be called 'tilt' funds, when a portfolio is tilted away from the index towards yield (by overweighting higher yielding stocks), or towards smaller companies (by overweighting shares of that kind); and so on. A tilt does not necessarily identify an inefficiency. An investor may actually want a higher yielding portfolio, irrespective of whether he expects to add value as compared with an ordinary index fund. But once a number of inefficiencies have been isolated, then active management can be reconstituted. It is important to remember that active management can entail quantitative methodologies: it is not only the judgemental, traditional managers that are active.

Since there are inefficiencies in markets – that is, situations which can be identified as not correctly discounting the future prospects of the shares involved – we have a very interesting line of development. A quantitative investment manager may find a number of inefficiencies – small companies, out of favour large companies, and so on – and combine them to put together a portfolio which, on a risk/return basis, will provide better results than an index fund. But this is just what the traditional investment analyst and portfolio management will do. What is the difference? Simply that the whole matter will have to be more systematic. Because of the high level of efficiency which will develop, the added value which can be achieved will not be very great. Mechanisms which can consistently provide 1 or 2 per cent over the averages will be seen as good. So it will be necessary to be systematic: without system, these very small added values will simply escape.

We have therefore in the US a situation in which the ideas of MPT are very well entrenched. The amount of money devoted to simple index matching has reached very large figures and is still growing sharply; the complex methodologies are coming into use. Also, the tide of these ideas is flowing around the world. On scientific grounds these theories are not a fad, or a fashion which will go away; they are based on reality and they will eventually (say, in five years?) conquer the whole world. In South Africa, for example, a number of investment professionals, aware of these approaches, nevertheless find very little interest in them amongst the major investors in the Republic. They should set all doubts on one side and ignore the views of the major clients and users of services. Those clients will come round to the MPT approach in due course and probably in the not very distant future. From the commercial point of view, the balance can be a nice one: to act too far ahead of the consensus is not to be understood; to ignore the ideas which will certainly become the consensus is to be shortsighted.

There are of course difficulties for the Efficient Market Theory, as the crash of 1987 showed. But although there is some difficulty in reconciling the efficiency of markets with that crash, and thus difficulties with that time period, all competing theories have trouble with all other time periods. It is important in these circumstances to treat what appears to be a contrary instance to a theory otherwise supported by massive evidence as a reason for looking more closely at the evidence and the logic, in order to complicate the theory (or perhaps make it more simple) and deal with the whole question at a greater level of sophistication. This is how science progresses. Anyone who dismisses the Efficient Market Theory on the basis of the crash of 1987 is proceeding in an unscientific manner. In any case, it is very difficult to see how markets could be as competitive as they are – that is, it is extremely difficult to out-perform consistently – unless information about shares is correctly discounted. It is easy to postulate a zero sum game about a realistic norm, it is very difficult to postulate a zero sum game around movements in prices which do not reflect reality. Not everyone, surely, can be so systematically mistaken. If so, one needs a theory of the madness of crowds so strong as to be impossible to believe. Such theories have been put forward and are worthy perhaps of a discussion on another occasion.

Let us summarise where the revolution lies in this (eventual) triumph of MPT. Investment managers always knew that the market was a difficult place, very competitive and difficult to beat. Now we know that this efficiency in pricing is fundamental. You cannot achieve above-average results unless your judgement is very good, very detached and very original. This rules out a very large number of people who are concerned in the business. Many of those involved are in fact doing something other than adding value – they may be wasting their time and the beneficiaries' money; they may be simply financial hand-holders (this is an extremely valuable and important task, as for example in the case of investment managers looking after private client money). But certainly a great deal of professionalism is required if a career is to be justified, and the methodologies of MPT provide for a professional basis on which to proceed: in the correct assessment and acceptance of risk; in the correct isolation of possible inefficiencies; and so on.

Incidentally, it can be argued that investment managers and analysts of little competence are in fact protected in their careers by an efficient market such as London. Because it is so easy to be right for the wrong reasons and wrong for the right reasons, it is sometimes difficult to see real analytical ability in an efficient market. Take an analyst to a very inefficient market, such as those which existed on the Continent until recently, and perhaps still do, and you will very soon find whether he or she is any good or not.

At this point, the argument can be broadened out to some extent. The new technology has led not only to the use of computers but to very rapid communications and therefore to the internationalisation of the investment problem. It is important to recognise how recently this has occurred. It is not very long ago when the fact that Japanese share prices appeared in the *Journal de Genève* was a matter for comment. Of course in principle it might appear that the internationalisation of the investment problem does not in itself change the nature of our business, simply extending the coverage, but in fact it does contribute to the revolution in two ways.

First, the change is so great a change of degree that it amounts to a change in kind. By the time you have taken account of the economic situation in so many overseas countries, and the impact of these changes on each other, and all the cultural differences such as accounting, most institutional investors (and, through them, private investors), are faced with an altogether larger series of opportunities and problems than in the purely domestic scene which existed until recently. But, secondly, there is a further element in this internationalisation. The amount of money which *has* flowed and, even more so, the amount of money which *will* flow from the great savings institutions such as those in the UK and the US, *to* the markets where opportunities are occurring – in many cases small, emerging markets – will in a certain timescale (perhaps five or seven years) make all the markets concerned efficient or close to it. In other words, the opportunities for investment will be 'ironed out'. Today, you can go to a foreign market and buy some very undervalued stocks, on Anglo-Saxon measures, or even on local measures; in a few years, this will not be possible any more.

What makes a market efficient? Obviously one needs a certain degree of efficiency in the purely technical sense, in that the stock exchange should be well organised and well regulated. There should also be sufficient liquidity; and a fairly constant population of investors. Markets where overseas investors come in from time to time but then leave from time to time might well suffer gross inefficiencies. Finally, of course, the investors in question must themselves have command of cash when required and be well informed. What the actual meaning of 'well informed' is remains to be discussed. It may be that investors in a particular market and at a particular time may have a level of information which, five years later, looks low: but nevertheless it is the consensus level of information at the time, and therefore the market can be efficient in the sense that it is difficult to out-perform the averages. It will not, of course, be as efficient at discounting the true future prospects of the shares as will be the case five years later.

Even these trends may leave some inefficiencies, of course. Small companies are often mentioned and certainly the small company area in the UK and the US still shows opportunities for above-average returns. But there are perhaps two elements in this. First, the lack of attention given to these small companies. It is certainly possible to argue, on the lines set out above, that this will change and that the amount of attention being given to these concerns will be greatly increased. Secondly, the consequent revaluations of small companies may still leave them providing a higher return than larger concerns. Or, to put it another way, the higher returns available on small companies will cease to be an inefficiency but become an efficiency, simply rewarding investors rather more for taking the rather higher risks for buying small companies. If this is the case, it is likely that the superior performance of shares in small companies will be rather lower than has been seen in the past. It should be noted as well that the small company effect can sometimes be negative for quite long periods; and that some commentators argue that the small company effect is in fact something of a statistical myth. (For a discussion of the 'small company' effect see, for example, E. Dimson (ed.) *Stock Market Anomalies,* CUP 1988.)

But there is still another way in which improved technology will lead to a revolution in investment management. It is simply that the whole problem of investment analysis and portfolio construction is being computerised. This is quite independent of any particular theories as to how it should be done. Databases are now being built up which will eventually cover every market in the world and virtually every share. There will be hundreds if not thousands of these databases and they will be updated with new information very rapidly. Thus even if the actual methods of investment analysis were not to change, the timescales involved in the various operations would be foreshortened to such an extent that for practical purposes we will be in a new environment.

Of course there are problems, and one of the main questions is that of standardising accounting rules internationally. So far the world can be said to be composed of quite good accounts, reasonably comparable already, in those countries which are traditionally stock exchange orientated. The leader in this field is of course the US although the UK with Canada, South Africa and Australia, for example is not far behind. These accounts are 'good' because they are aimed at the external user. On the other hand, on the continent of Europe and in particular in Germany, the external user has not until recently been a very important factor. Money in Germany has been raised in the banking parlours and the people in the banks know the true figures. Since this continental tradition is embodied to a large extent in the law, and since this general approach has been adopted by Brussels, we have a serious problem in dealing with the improvement of accounts in the European Community.

As regards the rest of the world – for example, in Japan – many problems will be solved if the Anglo-Saxon approach and the continental European approach can be reconciled. The difficulties are similar. Otherwise, many countries are simply catching up. The International Accounting Standards Committee (IASC) has been working for many years in setting accounting standards on the world level, and many developing countries have simply taken over the IASC standards *en bloc*, or to a large extent. In this work, incidentally, the IASC has taken account of the approaches and interests of the developing countries.

But all this might be considered a little ambitious – domestic constituencies in accounting questions are very powerful, not least the Commission of the European Communities (EC). Nevertheless with internationalisation of capital markets there has been an increasing demand for international co-ordination and things are going quite fast at the moment. This would not, however, be a very dramatic statement were it not for one relatively new factor: and that is that the International Organisation of Securities Commissions has taken an interest. Securities Commissions are the bodies in the various countries which control the listing requirements on the stock exchanges. Were bodies such as the SEC in the US to determine a move towards the internationalisation of accounting standards, whatever that move might be, the whole question of international standards would become more realistic. Note that one needs only a small move by the relevant bodies. As soon as that move is taken, companies and other interested parties around the world will begin to take the internationalisation of standards seriously. That in itself will accelerate the move towards further steps in that direction. There may therefore be a rather dramatic change in the situation for international accounting standards in the next year or two. If so, certain techniques of MPT, for example structuring portfolios through optimisation on the international level, will be very greatly facilitated.

It is problems such as accounting (and perhaps chiefly accounting), which lead to the conclusion that it might take another five or seven years before the revolution which has been outlined will actually come into being. But in something like that timescale, and in the absence of a worldwide depression which always slows things down, there will not be that much difference in the relatively near future between investing in London and investing in Norway and investing in Thailand and even, perhaps, investing in Vietnam. And it will all be computerised. This question of internationalisation, the increasing efficiency of all markets, and computerisation, is in a fundamental sense nothing very much to do with MPT. Markets will become more 'efficient' in the sense that so much investment expertise and money will be brought to bear that prices will be intensely competitive. Over and above that, of course, all the techniques of MPT will also be involved.

Some fairly serious qualifications to this forecast should be entered. First there will always be 'new' opportunities which will require something like the traditional approach. New flotations of shares for example, arbitrage in the takeover and merger market, and of course emerging countries – all of these will provide opportunities where the methodologies will not differ very much from what is going forward at the moment. A more important example is perhaps international asset allocation. Of course a proper analysis of risk both nationally and internationally is a valid and indeed necessary part of the asset allocation process and, subject to a refinement of the concept of risk, the theories and the technology are already in place. But asset allocation also requires a method of dealing with returns, and here a much greater problem exists. Governments and central banks all around the world are failing to forecast economic growth correctly and it seems unlikely that there can be a firm quantitative model to deal with the question of returns. Within a relatively closed economy – perhaps the US – something may be possible, but internationally judgement will still be very much the order of the day. What is puzzling, incidentally, is that the judgement of many fund managers has been so poor on the asset allocation between countries; since the amount of money flowing around the world is still not enough to make stock exchanges efficient with respect to each other, one would have thought that there would be an opportunity for above-average returns. But as you know many very serious mistakes have been made in allocating portfolios around the world.

Despite these qualifications – and they are important, of course – what one will see is an investment business which is systematised to a very high degree, and within a few years. Without such a systematic approach the investment manager will simply be too late in the vast majority of instances; and there will be nowhere in the world where he can go to apply the more traditional and slower techniques.

It might be asked how investment managers, and in particular investment managers positioned in the UK, should adapt themselves to these trends. And we are, of course, talking about the organisation of the business, the investment firms or the investment departments, who have some control of the commercial planning. First, obviously, the ideas of MPT must be taken on board. This implies recruiting or training and it also requires, to a degree varying according to the type of institution involved, the development of techniques rather ahead in many cases of what can be practically implemented. There is so much going on that a good deal of work needs to be done in advance of its practical implementation.

This implementation will itself lead to the development of databases and computer techniques. But it would be best to look at computer operations in a broader context. Systems which grow like Topsy are likely to be a bad investment later on. It is better to sit down now and decide on the mechanisms which will be required and, of course, to integrate them with the similar developments which are going ahead on the administrative and back office sides. Indeed, it can be said that one element in these developments is that the back office and the front office will become very much merged.

In carrying this out, it is important to look upon the changes not as an introduction only of MPT but the computerisation of traditional methods. This too must be thought out objectively and it will involve a number of databases, some of which do not yet exist. It would also be extremely valuable if large investment institutions of all kinds would take an interest in the solving of some of the problems which are necessary in the establishment of these databases – for example, money and volunteers are required to solve the international accounting standards problems.

None of these will seem very interesting developments to the well established team of fund managers working in the traditional way. But they are sitting on a time-bomb and it is the job of management to make these moves and to persuade the practitioners to move accordingly. This may, of course, be easier if performance is not very good; and it should be remembered that although above-average performance is very difficult to achieve in efficient markets it is very easy to eliminate below-average performance, if only by adopting a simple index matched approach. More and more, this is an argument that is having an impact in the US.

Taking all these forecasts together, investment might perhaps seem rather dull. But I do not think that is the case. Whereas the idea of making an enormous amount of money very quickly has to recede as markets become more efficient, the tools that will be available for the correct structuring of portfolios, within markets and across markets, will on the other hand be sophisticated and more and more complicated. Risk and return will be able to be matched to an investor's needs, and a complex series of decisions will make up the investment exercise. A great deal of judgement and work will be necessary not in choosing ICI rather than Shell, but in working the whole machine and putting portfolios together in an appropriate way. The change will be as different as chemistry was from alchemy, and I think that that can be called a revolution.

2 An Introduction to Capital Protection Strategies

Andrew Perrins

INTRODUCTION

The rapid growth of derivative instruments over the last decade has enabled investors to develop strategies which were not possible before. Undoubtedly the most controversial of these are strategies which aim to protect an investor's capital against loss of value – commonly known as portfolio insurance strategies. Early in 1987 these strategies were being acclaimed as the way forward for pension fund investment, particularly in the US where new accounting regulations had come into force. Later that same year they were in some quarters being blamed for the October crash.

This paper looks at the two main types of capital protection strategy – how they work and the pros and cons of each. But the first question is: why have these strategies become so popular?

THE ATTRACTION OF CAPITAL PROTECTION STRATEGIES

Over the last seventy years UK equities have outperformed both cash and gilts by over 6 per cent p.a.[1] Most investors expect equities to out-perform other asset types in the future. It is therefore understandable that investors should wish to commit as large a percentage to equities as their risk tolerance allows. But what is risk tolerance? How is it expressed? In the real world there are many investors whose attitudes to risk cannot be defined in the traditional way – in terms of the variability of anticipated returns. They have a bottom line – a minimum return which must be achieved. It is to these investors that capital protection strategies appeal.

Capital protection strategies permit investors to gain greater exposure to equity assets than they could tolerate without such strategies. They are most appropriate to organisations with short-term liabilities or to investors with short-term investment objectives.

An organisation with long-term liabilities, such as a UK final salary pension scheme, can tolerate far greater investment risk. A growing fund can meet its current obligations out of its regular income, and has no need to realise assets at their current market value. Short-term fluctuations in equity values are therefore of little concern. A large part of the fund can be invested in equities, and portfolio protection is unlikely to be necessary. This is not so, however, in the US, where the view formed of a pension fund's solvency can be heavily dependent on market values. In 1987 new accounting regulations (FASB 87) came into force. The effect of these was to show changes on the surplus of the fund in the corporate balance sheet and income statement.[2] It was this accounting standard that was responsible for the huge growth in popularity of 'portfolio insurance' in America in 1987, and by October it was estimated that $60bn–$90bn of US funds were managed in this way.[3]

OPTIONS STRATEGIES

There are two main approaches which fall under this heading, one using call options (commonly known as the 90:10 method), the other using put options. We now need to look at the way in which they work.

The 90:10 Method

Consider an investor with £100m who requires at least the return of his capital after one year, but wishes to participate in equity gains over the period. If one-year money is earning just over 11 per cent he can guarantee the return of his capital by putting £90m on deposit at this rate. The other £10m is invested in call options to capture equity market returns. This is where the term '90:10' comes from. In practice, the interest rate will be different and the investor's time horizon may be more or less than one year. The percentage invested in cash or bonds will be fixed accordingly, so as to ensure that the minimum acceptable return is achieved.

Hedging With Put Options

An alternative to holding cash and call options is to hold stocks and put options. Consider the investor with £100m who requires at least the return of his capital after one year. He buys a one-year stock index put option, with an exercise price equal to the current market level. If this costs 4 per cent, he can invest £96m in the stocks constituting the index. The put option protects the portfolio from falling in value below £96m while dividend income brings the value back up to its original £100m. If the stocks rise in value, the investor captures 96 per cent of stock market gains, but obviously loses the original £4m invested in options.

Graphical Representation

Consider a portfolio, value £100, current market index level 100.

Let x be the market index return excluding dividends
d be dividends receivable at the end of the year
i be the riskless rate of return
c be the premium required to buy a call option, expiring at year end, strike price 100, giving a return of $x - c$
y be the return, measured in £t, from a portfolio of £100

90:10 Method

For cash,	$y = i$	
For a call option,	$y = \quad -c$	if $x<0$
	$y = x - c$	if $x>0$
For the 90:10 method	$y = 0.9i - 10$	if $x<0$
	$y = 0.9i - 10 + 10x/c$	if $x>0$

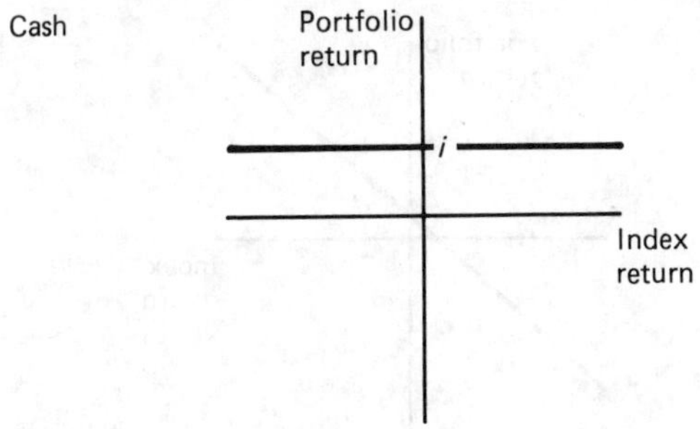

Call Options

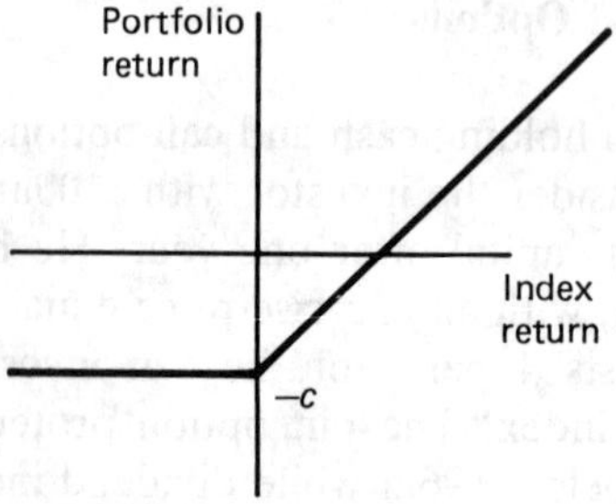

Cash and
Call Options

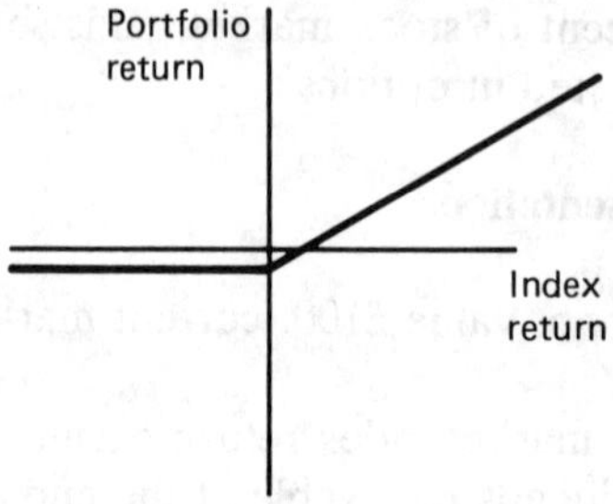

Hedging With Put Options

Let p be the premium required to buy put options, strike price 100, sufficient to protect a portfolio of size (100-p)

For a fully invested portfolio	$y = x + d$	
For a put option	$y = -x-p$ if $x<0$	
	$y = -p$ if $x>0$	
For the protected portfolio	$y = (100-p)(100+d)/100-100$	if $x<0$
	$y = (100-p)(100+x+d)/100-100$	if $x>0$

Stocks

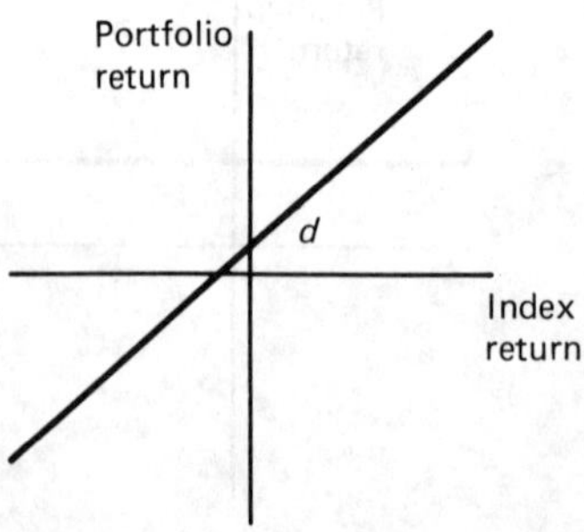

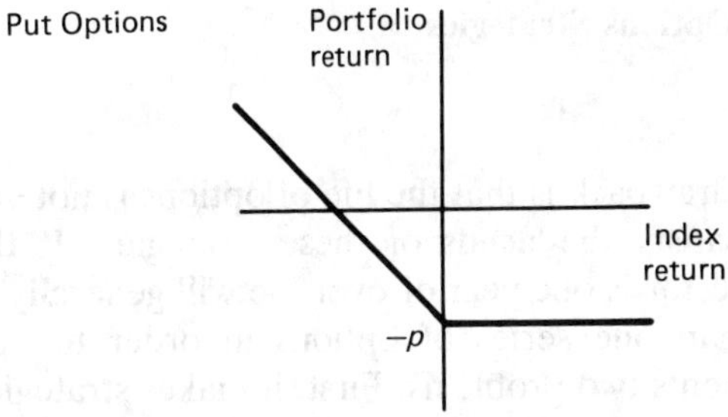

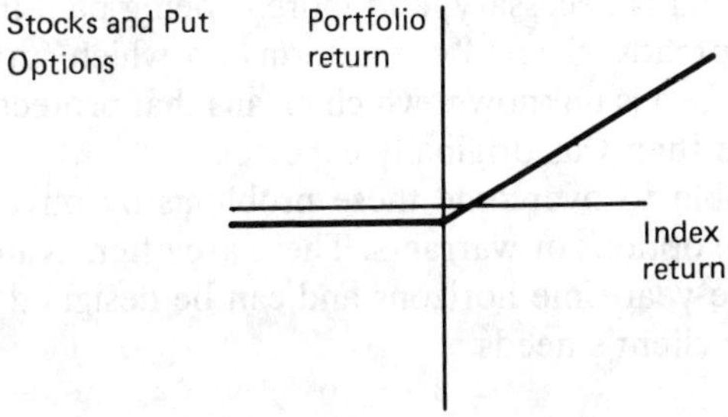

Advantages of Options Strategies

Guaranteed Minimum Returns

The main advantage of options strategies is the certainty that the portfolio value will not fall below a certain level – we will see later that the dynamic hedging method offers only a strong probability that this will be achieved, but options strategies can guarantee the minimum return, because the risk is underwritten by the writer of the option (with an index put strategy, the guarantee holds only if the stocks actually held do not under-perform the index).

Predictability of Returns

The final value of the portfolio depends only on the final value of the index. This contrasts with the dynamic hedging approach, where the return depends on how the index moved during the period.

Ease of Day-to-day Management

Once an option strategy has been put in place and the options purchased, the manager can sit back and await the results. Further activity is necessary only to manage cashflows or if options expire.

Disadvantages of Options Strategies

Length of Options

The most serious drawback is that the life of options is not generally long enough to satisfy the needs of these strategies. If the time horizon of the investor is one year or over, he will generally need to purchase more than one series of options in order to effect his strategy. This presents two problems. First, it makes strategies more expensive than they need otherwise be, because more protection is being purchased than is necessary, and more is being paid in way of commission and spreads. Secondly, the terms on which further options can be purchased is unknown, which means that protection may be more expensive than was originally expected.

It may be possible to overcome these problems by buying over-the-counter (OTC) options or warrants. These are often available for one-, two- or three-year time horizons and can be designed so as to meet precisely the client's needs.

Tracking Error

A strategy of holding stocks and stock index put options will achieve the expected returns only if the stocks held perform in line with the index. In particular, if the market suffers a large fall and the stocks held under-perform the index, then the floor return will not be achieved. This risk can be minimised by controlling the tracking error of stocks held compared to the index, or by buying individual stock options instead of index options. However, individual stock options will generally be more expensive, because (a) expiry dates are shorter and (b) volatilities are larger.

Expected Returns

One advantage of options strategies already mentioned is that returns are not path-dependent. For any given market return, the expected return from an option strategy can be calculated in advance. For example, consider an investor with £100m in FTSE stocks. He buys £5.5m of FTSE put options, with an exercise price equal to 100 per cent of the current index level and a premium of 5.5 per cent. This puts a floor of £100m on the stocks held, in addition to the £4.4m he expects to receive in dividend payments (assumed for simplicity to be received at the end of the year). He thus establishes a 99 per cent

Table 2.1 Returns and 'upside capture': various levels of equity market return

Total FTSE return (%)	*Final value of portfolio (£m)*	*Return on portfolio (%)*	*Upside capture (%)*
–20	104.4	–1.0	N/A
–10	104.4	–1.0	N/A
0	104.4	–1.0	Negative
5	105.0	–0.5	Negative
10	110.0	4.3	43
15	115.0	9.0	60
20	120.0	13.7	69
30	130.0	23.2	77
40	140.0	32.7	82

floor (£104.4m on his initial investment of £105.5m).

The returns and 'upside capture' expected for various levels of equity market return are shown in Table 2.1. 'Upside capture' is defined as the return from a protected portfolio as a percentage of the return from a fully invested portfolio.

DYNAMIC HEDGING

Origins

When Professor Hayne Leland from the University of Berkeley, California took his sabbatical in 1977, it was suggested to him that it would be of real economic value to society if he could find a way of insuring against stock market losses. His answer was to develop a strategy of systematically buying and selling stock known as dynamic hedging – a strategy which became so popular that as we have seen by October 1987 an estimated $60 – $90bn of equity assets were managed in this way.

The Principles of Dynamic Hedging

The starting point is to decide on a 'floor' – the minimum acceptable value for the portfolio. At any time the difference between the actual value of the portfolio and the floor is known as the 'cushion'. The portfolio itself is split into two parts – risky assets (usually equities) and safe assets (usually cash on deposit or short-dated fixed interest securities). The percentage held in risky assets is known as the exposure. As the fund value increases, the cushion increases, giving greater freedom to invest in risky assets (i.e., increasing the exposure). As the fund value falls the cushion decreases, and the exposure has to be reduced until as the cushion approaches zero the exposure approaches zero. In other words, by the time the fund value reaches the floor the fund is 100 per cent invested in safe assets.

Some forms of dynamic hedging use complex mathematical models to determine the asset mix, calculating the exposure to replicate synthetically the behaviour of a put option.[4] This makes dynamic hedging more complicated than it needs to be. It is more common for the exposure to be determined from a simple formula of the form:

$e = mc$
e = exposure (amount in the risky asset)
c = cushion (fund value minus floor)
m = multiple (controls the sensitivity)

Dynamic hedging using a formula of this type is known as 'Constant Proportion Portfolio Insurance' (CPPI).

Practical Application

'Tolerance'

In practice, market values will fluctuate, and the cushion and target exposure will vary. It would clearly be very expensive constantly to rebalance the portfolio to achieve target exposure, as the fund would be subject to a 'whipsaw' effect of buying high and selling low. It is far wiser to rebalance only at a certain 'trigger' point, either when the market has moved by a certain amount since the last rebalance, or when the actual exposure differs from the target exposure by more than a specified amount. The degree by which the market moves or the exposure diverges from target before triggering a trade is known as the 'tolerance'.

Multiple

The choice of multiple determines the degree of risk taken. A small multiple gives a low exposure to equities, and a very small chance that the fund value will ever reach the floor. A larger multiple gives a higher exposure to equities, but increases the chance that the fund value will fall through the floor. For instance, consider an investor with a fund of 100, a floor of 95, and a multiple of 4. His cushion is 5 and he will invest his fund 20/80 equities/cash. There is very little chance that his chosen floor will be threatened. If, however, he had chosen a multiple of 20 he would have invested 100 in equities. If the market suddenly fell by over 5 per cent and he was unable to sell during the fall, his floor would be breached.

Stock Index Futures

In practice, rebalancing will normally be carried out using stock index futures rather than the physical stocks, for reasons of speed and cost. By buying a stock index future the investor gains an immediate exposure to every stock in the index. The transaction is completed in seconds, removing the problem of deciding which individual stocks to buy and sell and saving the time (which can be of vital importance when sales are triggered) of dealing in those stocks. Furthermore the market impact of dealing in futures is likely to be less than dealing in the underlying stocks.

The transaction costs associated with dealing in futures are far smaller than dealing in the underlying stocks. A round-trip transaction (i.e., buying and selling) would typically cost less than 0.2 per cent in the future, compared to nearly 2 per cent in the underlying stocks. When dealing in futures, there is a further 'cost' which is not known at outset, and may be positive or negative, depending on whether the future is trading cheaply or expensively compared with its 'fair value'.

Advantages of Dynamic Hedging

Flexibility

The dynamic hedging method is very flexible. A change of strategy in mid-term (e.g., a change of floor or an increased multiple) can be accommodated immediately, simply by buying or selling the appropriate number of futures contracts. Furthermore the strategy can from the outset be operated with a static or a moving floor. Consider these examples:

(a) An investor with 100 to invest wants to be able to stop the strategy at any time with the return of at least 90.

In this case, the floor is fixed at 90.

(b) An investor with 100 to invest requires that at least 110 will be available at the end of three years.

In this case the floor is

$110/(1+i)^{3-t/12}$

where t is time in months

i is the interest rate to the end of year 3

In other words if the floor is reached before the end of the three years, the fund will be fully invested in cash, and will grow to 110 by the end of the period.

Higher Expected Returns

An options strategy requires another party to underwrite the risk on the options purchased. A dynamic hedging strategy takes the risk of being unable to deal in sufficient size at the appropriate time in order to protect the floor. This should give higher expected returns because the fund is not paying the 'certainty premium' that would be implicit in the price of an option.

Longer Time Horizons

Option strategies are limited by the non-availability of longer-dated options. Dynamic hedging allows the creation of strategies with longer time horizons than are feasible using options.

Disadvantages of Dynamic Hedging

Risk of 'Failure'

There are two fundamental objections to this strategy. First, there is no *guarantee* that a dynamic strategy will protect the floor return. The fund is itself bearing the risk of a sharp decline in equity prices during which it is not possible to deal in the required size. This risk increases as the multiple (m) used in the formula increases, but the biggest danger is that the size of the equity market decline is itself exacerbated by the weight of money following similar strategies. The Brady Report, commissioned after the October 1987 crash, estimated that dynamic hedging led to sales of $20bn–$30bn of shares between 14 and 20 October and, additionally, short-term traders sold shares heavily in anticipation of dynamic hedging sales. The Report concluded that dynamic hedging was a major reason for the unprecedented speed with which markets fell.

The 'Whipsaw' Effect

The second fundamental objection is that the dynamic hedging process involves buying after prices have risen and selling after prices have fallen. This would appear contrary to common sense, and if markets are volatile the strategy is subject to a 'whipsaw effect' where the manager is obliged to sell stocks at a lower price than he bought them at, or buy at a higher price that he sold at. This must clearly result in diminished returns.

Uncertainty

A lesser problem is that of uncertainty. The returns from a dynamic strategy are dependent not only on the returns from the safe and risky assets, but also on the way in which the fund's exposure to those assets moves over the period and the pattern of market returns during the period. For example, if the equity market rose steadily throughout the year to return gains of 40 per cent a dynamic strategy would show a healthy return, but if the market initially fell sharply and then recovered strongly to return 40 per cent on the year as a whole, the dynamic strategy would show a poor return. This is because the initial fall will leave the fund with a low exposure to equities, and consequently only a small proportion of the fund will benefit from the subsequent rise.

Simulating the Returns From Dynamic Hedging Strategies

Many studies have used historical results to present expected returns from a dynamic hedging strategy. These studies serve an important role in showing the historical behaviour of protection strategies. However, historical research is limited by the amount of historic data available, and does not allow the exploration of all possibilities in terms of the pattern of equity market returns. For this kind of information one has to turn to stochastic modelling. To examine the returns from different dynamic hedging strategies one needs to make an assumption about the probability distribution of equity market returns. I have assumed that the shape of returns is best represented by the log-normal distribution. In practice returns may not follow this distribution, but the impact on results is unlikely to be large.

The Formula Used

The formula[5], I have used in simulations is of the form:

$$e = mc - t$$

where t is the tolerance
e is the % of the current fund invested in equities
m is the multiple
c is the current fund value minus the floor, expressed as a % of the current fund value

Two features of the formula should be noted.

First the cushion has been expressed as a percentage of the current fund value. If the actual exposure is equal to mc, the cushion will not be eroded (the floor will not be breached) unless the market falls by over $100/m$ per cent *and* the manager is unable to deal in sufficient size during the fall. This is very helpful because it quantifies the risk of the protection failing. Secondly, by defining the *target* exposure as $e = mc - t$ we ensure that the *actual* exposure will never exceed mc. Hence the model can always withstand a rapid fall of $100/m$ per cent, even when the actual exposure is t per cent above the target exposure.

Assumptions Needed

The return from a dynamic strategy is dependent on a number of factors, some within the control of the 'designer' of the strategy, some outside his control. Assumptions are required for the following:

Factors within the investor's control

- Time horizon of the strategy.
- Degree of protection required (i.e., floor return).
- Multiple chosen in the formula.
- Tolerance permitted before rebalancing.

Factors outside the investor's control

- Returns on safe asset (cash).
- Returns on risky asset (equity).
- Volatility/pattern of returns on equity.
- Transaction expenses/futures mispricing.

Central Assumptions

The central assumptions used in the simulations are as follows:

Time horizon	One year
Floor	100% of initial fund value
Multiple	5
Tolerance	5%
Return on safe assets	10% p.a.
Mean return on equity	15% p.a.
Volatility	18%
Rebalancing costs	0.5%

Notes to Assumptions

1. The floor value must be available at the end of the time horizon. Hence after time t (in years) the floor is

$$100/(1 + i)^{1-t}$$

where i is the return on safe assets.
2. A multiple of 5 implies that the strategy is able to withstand a rapid equity market decline of 20 per cent.
3. Tolerance of 5 per cent means that the portfolio will be rebalanced when actual exposure diverges from target exposure by more than 5 per cent.
4. Volatility is measured by the annualised standard deviation of equity market returns. The figure of 18 per cent compares with volatility of 18–22 per cent experienced in the equity markets of the UK, the US and Japan over the period 1984–9 (or 14–18 per cent if the third quarter of 1987 is excluded).
5. Rebalancing costs of 0.5 per cent assume that rebalancing is carried out using futures. An allowance is included for adverse mispricing of the future relative to the index.

Results

Table 2.2 and Figure 2.1 show the results of simulations following the central assumptions outlined above.

Table 2.2 Equity market returns and expected returns

Equity market returns		*Expected return from protected portfolio*	
Range (%)	*Probability (%)*	*Mean return (%)*	*Upside capture (%)*
<0	20.6	3.4	N/A
0–2	3.8	5.0	500
2–4	4.1	5.6	186
4–6	4.3	5.8	117
6–8	4.5	6.4	91
8–10	4.5	7.1	79
10–12	4.6	7.5	68
12–14	4.6	8.1	63
14–16	4.3	9.0	60
16–20	8.4	9.7	54
20–30	16.9	12.9	52
30–40	10.4	18.7	53
40–50	5.3	25.8	57
> 50	3.7	40.2	67
Mean arithmetic returns (%)		*10.9*	*73*
Mean geometric returns (%)		*10.6*	*71*

Central Assumptions

Expected equity return	= 15% p.a.	Multiple	= 5
Marketed volatility	= 18% p.a.	Tolerance	= 5%
Riskless rate	= 10% p.a.	Floor	= 100%

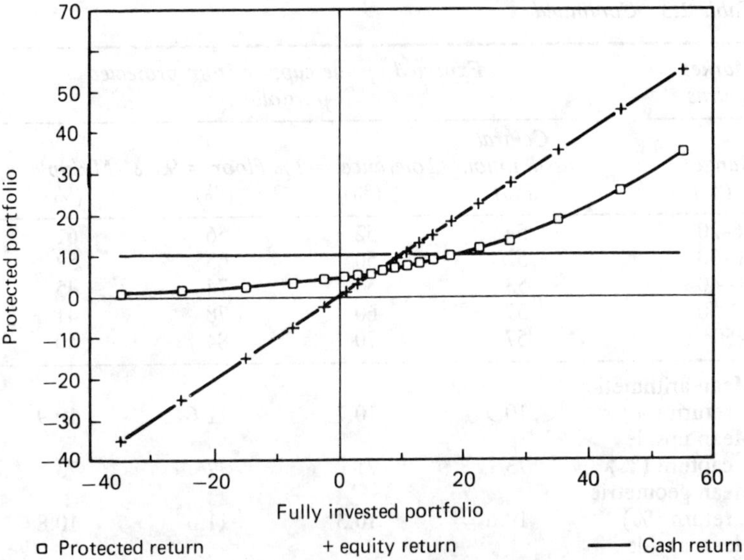

Source: Abbey Life
Figure 2.1 Dynamic hedging over a one-year period

The Effect of Factors Within the Investor's Control

Table 2.3 and Figure 2.2 show the effect of changing just one of the central assumptions.

Table 2.3 Market returns and expected 'upside capture': factors within the investor's control

Market returns	*Expected upside capture from protected portfolio*			
Range (%)	*Central assumptions (%)*	*Tolerance = 2% (%)*	*Floor = 95% (%)*	*Multiple = 3 (%)*
0–2	500	444	200	770
2–4	186	167	98	270
4–6	117	108	71	165
6–8	91	84	63	123
8–10	79	74	59	101
10–12	68	65	59	88
12–14	63	60	58	77
14–16	60	57	56	70

continued on page 34

Table 2.3 Continued

Market returns	*Expected upside capture from protected portfolio*			
Range (%)	*Central assumptions (%)*	*Tolerance = 2% (%)*	*Floor = 95% (%)*	*Multiple = 3 (%)*
16–20	54	52	56	61
20–30	52	50	63	52
30–40	53	54	74	45
40–50	57	60	78	41
>50	57	70	84	40
Mean arithmetic return (%)	10.9	10.7	11.6	10.9
Mean upside capture (%)	73	71	77	73
Mean geometric return (%)	10.6	10.3	11.0	10.8
Mean upside capture (%)	71	69	73	72

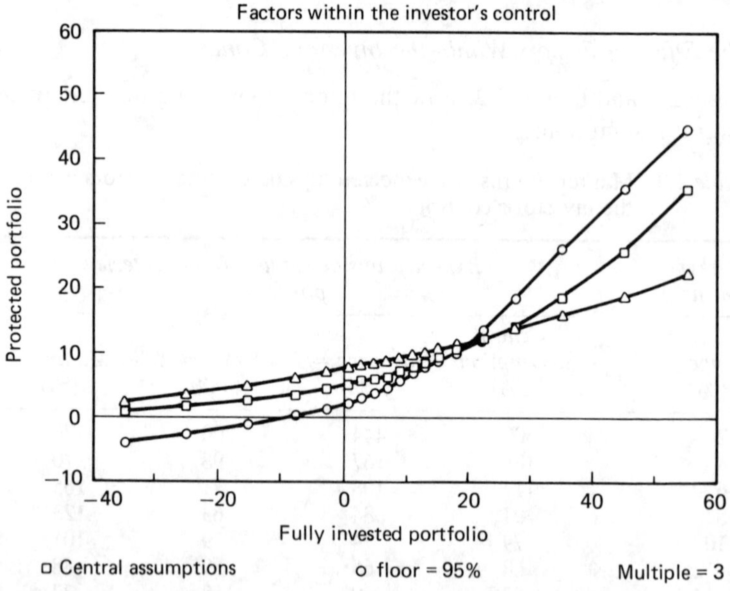

Source: Abbey Life

Figure 2.2 Returns from dynamic hedging strategies: factors within the investor's control

The Effect of Factors Outside the Investor's Control

Table 2.4 and Figure 2.3 demonstrate this.

Table 2.4 Market returns and expected 'upside capture': factors outside the investor's control

Market returns	*Expected upside capture from protected portfolio*		
Range (%)	*Central assumptions (%)*	*Riskless rate = 12% (%)*	*Volatility = 25% p.a. (%)*
0–2	500	535	385
2–4	186	200	133
4–6	117	126	88
6–8	91	100	70
8–10	79	85	58
10–12	68	75	51
12–14	63	69	49
14–16	60	66	46
16–20	54	61	38
20–30	52	58	40
30–40	53	60	41
40–50	57	65	48
> 50	67	74	56
Mean arithmetic return (%)	10.9	12.1	8.6
Mean upside capture (%)	73	81	57
Mean geometric return (%)	10.6	11.8	8.4
Mean upside capture (%)	71	79	56

Comment on the Factors Affecting Results

Factors within the investor's control

A tolerance level of 2 per cent instead of 5 per cent allows a higher initial exposure to equities, and maintains a higher exposure as prices trend upwards. Consequently, this gives a higher upside capture when equity markets show a strong rise. However, the lower tolerance results in more 'whipsawing' taking place, and if equity returns are only moderate the cost of 'whipsawing' outweighs the benefit of a higher equity exposure.

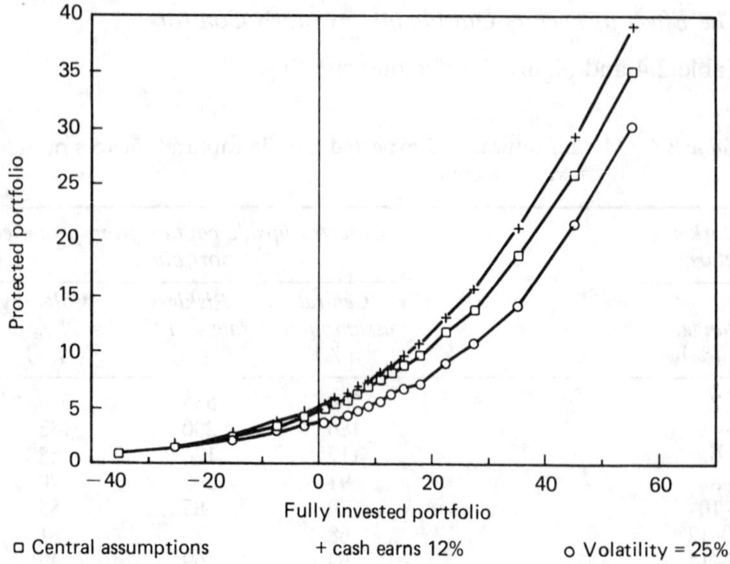

Source: Abbey Life

Figure 2.3 Returns from dynamic hedging strategies: factors outside the investor's control

A lower floor or a higher multiple both have the effect of increasing the exposure to equities. As a result they both lead to higher returns when equities do well. A lower multiple reduces the sensitivity of the model, making it less vulnerable to whipsaw. It is interesting that although the comparison between a multiple of 5 and one of 3 shows the same mean arithmetic return, the model with the lower multiple gives a higher geometric return, indicating a smaller dispersion of likely returns.

Factors outside the investor's control

A higher return on cash naturally gives a higher return overall. However, in the case where the riskless rate is 12 per cent, the mean return relative to cash is very disappointing. The incremental return from investing partly in equity has been eroded by transaction costs, in this case, a higher expected return from equities is needed to make portfolio protection look attractive. High equity market volatility results in high dealing costs unless the mutiple chosen is sufficiently low to compensate. In the example shown, with equities expected to out-perform by 5 per cent but with a volatility of 25 per cent, the expected return is lower than that from cash.

CONCLUSIONS

Capital protection strategies do not improve the traditional risk/return comparison. Instead they substitute one return distribution for another so as to suit the investor's risk preference. With dynamic hedging strategies there is still a small chance that the floor return will not be achieved. This will occur if a sudden large equity market decline is experienced, during which time the investor is unable to sell in sufficient quantity to reduce the exposure to the required level. Dynamic strategies rely on the liquidity of futures markets, and will yield disappointing returns if the volume of money following these strategies is too large. In the extreme, this can lead to *acute* price corrections such as were seen in October 1987. High volatility in markets leads to a 'whipsawing' effect of buying high and selling low, which depresses returns.

Despite these problems, dynamic hedging can still be a useful tool if the following provisos are observed:

(a) The risky asset used should be one in which other dynamic hedgers are not over-active.
(b) The investor should have a full understanding of the risks involved.
(c) The formula employed must be chosen carefully, reflecting the investor's attitude towards risk and his expectation of market return and volatility.

Options strategies can give the investor an absolute guarantee that the floor return will be achieved. They are far simpler to operate than dynamic hedging strategies, but are less flexible. It may be difficult to construct a viable strategy for longer time horizons because the required instruments may not be available.

Capital protection strategies have a definite role to play in the investment planning of shorter-term investors. The derivative product industry has seen huge growth over the last ten years, which has encouraged the growth of capital protection strategies, over the next ten years we will see further growth and innovation in derivative products, and further growth and innovation in the application of capital protection techniques.

Notes

1. From the 'BZW Equity-Gilt Study' (January 1989).
2. See S. P. Somes and M. A. Zurack, 'Pension Plans, Portfolio Insurance and FASB Statement No 87', *Financial Analysts' Journal* (January–February 1987).
3. 'The Report of the Presidential Task Force on Market Mechanisms' (The Brady Report) (January 1988).
4. See F. Black and R. Rouhani, 'Constant Proportion Portfolio Insurance and the Synthetic Put Option: A Comparison', Goldman Sachs Research (May 1987).
5. The formula is of the CPPI type. The results of simulating a synthetic put option strategy can be found in R. G. Clarive and R. D. Arnott, 'The Cost of Portfolio Insurance: Tradeoffs and Choices', *Financial Analysts' Journal* (November–December 1987).

3 Asset Allocation: A Case Study

Jane Platt

Since the theme of this conference has been the investigation of some of the theories of investment, I will be taking a selection of these theories and showing how they have been applied. I am interested in what is of practical use in solving investors' problems and, indeed, what is generally acceptable to investors. New ideas are not always readily acceptable in this field. Most people are very cautious when it comes to money, particularly when they are responsible for other peoples'.

Efficient frontier techniques are not particularly new but they are still relatively rare in terms of the numbers of clients of UK investment houses using them. The case study we will look at concerns one of the first clients whose assets we began to manage on such a basis. The details of the fund have been disguised to protect the client's anonymity.

The story starts four years ago, half way around the world. The Hong Kong market was going through one of its periodic bouts of volatility and the people of Hong Kong were going through one of their periodic bouts of uncertainty about what would happen in 1997. This combination of events sparked some important ideas in the mind of a far-sighted manager in charge of a major Hong Kong pension fund. He decided that the traditional way of managing Hong Kong pension funds, in Hong Kong, was just too risky. He was worried that even keeping the assets in Hong Kong was potentially dangerous. Far better to have the assets out of harm's way in the safe hands of an overseas custodian. He approached Barclays in the Channel Islands to provide custodian services. One of our directors was sorting out the details of an offshore client in Jersey at the time. When the enquiry arrived, he saw that it would make sense to manage the money away from Hong Kong too. He asked Barclays to see whether an investment management proposal would interest the client. It would.

Two weeks later we were sitting in the manager's Hong Kong office to discuss the fund's objectives. The notes arising from the meeting looked like this:

Size of fund	HK$ 400m
Maturity profile	No liabilities for 20 years
Current management	Aggressive, active with traditional asset allocation deviating little from the consensus of Hong Kong funds
Goals	1. Minimise risk of having to realise the assets of the fund at short notice because of any political changes
	2. Safeguard assets from being frozen in Hong Kong if the law was changed
	3. Minimise costs of reorganisation
	4. Decide objective performance benchmarks

It seemed to us that the asset allocation techniques that we were developing, using *efficient frontier* technology, would be perfect for such a client. But four years ago it was virtually unknown in the UK pension fund community, far less in Hong Kong.

DEFINING RISK

The reason why we thought efficient frontier techniques would be particularly appropriate was the way in which we were measuring risk. In our model, risk was defined as the historic volatility of a market. We compiled the figures over a standard period for each market, in practice this meant over the period for which we had data for the most recently monitored market. Why was volatility an appropriate measure of risk for this Hong Kong fund? The Trustees' main concern was that they would have to realise their assets at short notice due to a change in the political outlook of the colony. Thus controlling short-term volatility would be most important. Imagine the consequences for a fund predominately invested in the Hong Kong market which was a forced seller in October 1987, the time of the crash.

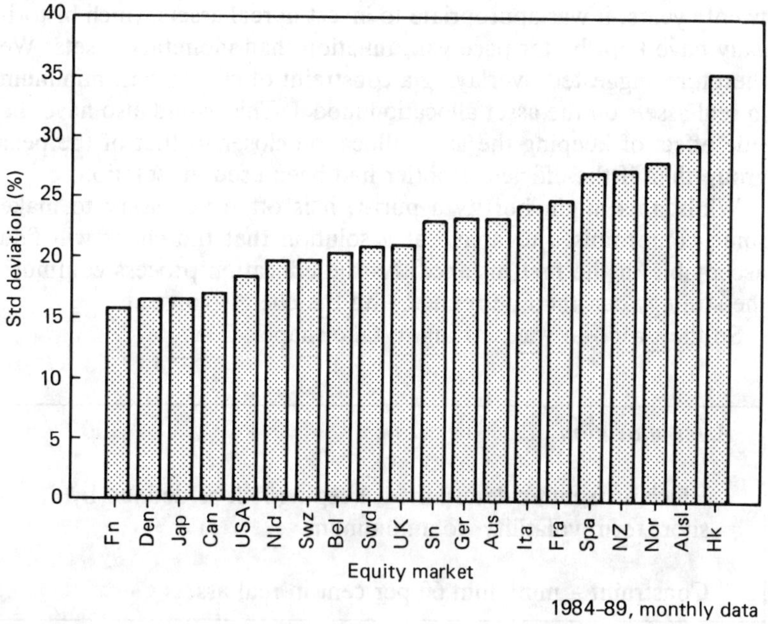

Source: BZW
Figure 3.1 Market volatilities

This definition of risk was also very different from that used by the incumbent managers, who saw risk as volatility of return against the peer group – that is, business risk to themselves as a fund management house in producing a return different from the consensus. Thus, if the Trustees decided to split the fund between the incumbents and ourselves, the two approaches would provide further diversification.

The volatilities of different markets do vary susbtantially. Figure 3.1 shows the volatilities of major markets based on five years' performance.

At the moment, the use of market volatility as the measure of risk in efficient frontier models is standard, whilst this short-term measure of risk may be appropriate for the effectively short-term objectives of the Hong Kong fund in question, it is not really appropriate to use when looking at the long-term benchmark of a conventional UK pension fund. Defining risk in a useful way in this context is a serious practical problem.

Having decided on the most appropriate measure of risk, we then looked at the liability profile of the fund. With no liabilities for twenty years, it was appropriate to invest in real assets which historically have kept better pace with inflation than monetary assets. We therefore suggested overlaying a constraint of 60 per cent minimum in real assets on the asset allocation model. This would also have the side effect of keeping the asset allocation closer to that of the peer group than if the efficient frontier had been used in isolation.

Whilst this might horrify a purist, it is often necessary to make some compromises to arrive at a solution that the client will find acceptable in the first instance. As the education process continues the strategy can then be refined with the client's consent.

So the proposal was starting to take shape:

Asset allocation

Efficient frontier determined, keeping risk as defined by short-term volatility, to a minimum.

Constraint – minimum 60 per cent in real assets

So far, so straightforward.

CREATING THE EFFICIENT FRONTIER

In practice, even at this stage, a high level of expertise is necessary to implement such a strategy. To create the efficient frontier, two basic sets of data are required:

1. Data on risk.
2. Forecasts for markets.

At first sight it would appear that 1 is objective and subjective. In practice, however, subjective analysis of both data and forecasts is necessary.

As we saw above, the risk data on the volatility of markets has to be for the same period for each market. At the time, we have five years' data for each of the major markets. The data is based on monthly performance figures and the risk is measured in terms of standard deviation. But the bald statistics have to be used with

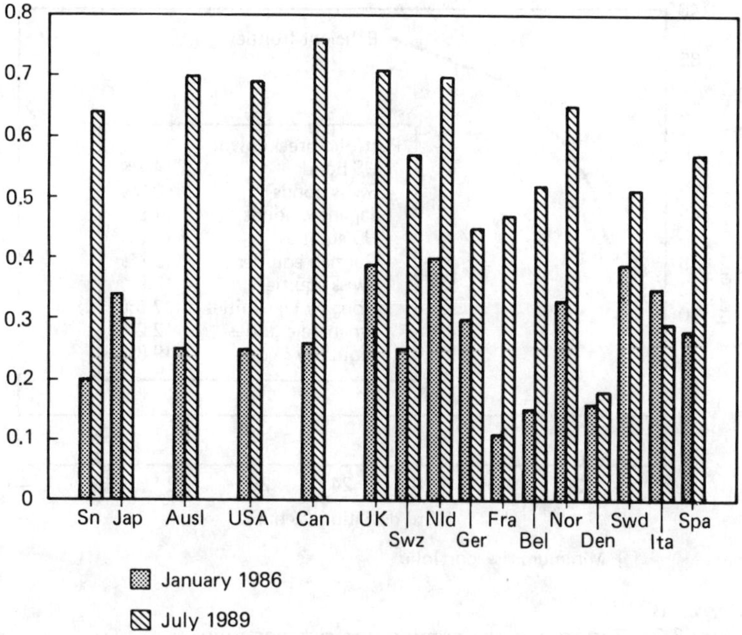

Source: BZW
Figure 3.2 Equity market correlations with Hong Kong

caution. An example of a typical problem arose in a BZW office. Our data showed no risk in investing in the US$ for a Hong Kong investor because the HK$ was pegged to the US currency. As an investment house, we considered that the future of the peg was in jeopardy. To use the historic data which showed no risk, or volatility, in US$ investments for a Hong Kong investor would therefore have been inconsistent. So even the risk data has to be subjectively assessed. There is considerably more to the implementation of quantitative techniques than can be handled by even the most skilled computer operator without extensive stock market knowledge.

How stable would the asset allocation be? That would depend on the forecasts and market correlations. Looking at the correlations between markets, they have changed, but the changes have tended to be consistent. Figure 3.2 is based on five-year, monthly data.

Figure 3.2 shows that the correlation between the behaviour of the Hong Kong market and other stock markets worldwide has steadily increased over the period 1987–9. This is no doubt a function of the

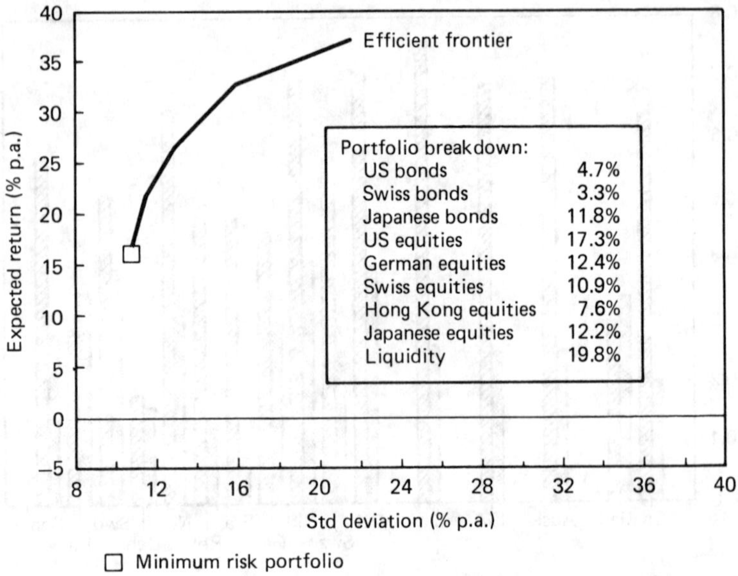

Source: BZW
Figure 3.3 Portfolio analysis: minimum risk portfolio

globalisation of markets and investor outlook, coupled with the effects of the crash. The currency peg to the US$ should not be significant in this context, as it has been in existence since October 1983.

This opens the interesting question of whether trends towards a global economy will eventually make the differences between the behaviour of individual markets so small that the opportunities for adding value through asset allocation will be seriously diminished. In fact, it is possible to determine the minimum risk asset allocation without the use of forecasts. This minimum risk portfolio could be used as the long-term benchmark against which the client could measure the success of our tactical asset allocation strategy. It would have looked like Figure 3.3.

Earlier I stated that we did require forecasts. This is because we believe that we can add value by using our forecasting ability. Of course, the minimum risk portfolio is the bottom left point on any full efficient frontier chart. In practice, this tends to vary only slightly over time.

Investment management houses used to have strategy committees.

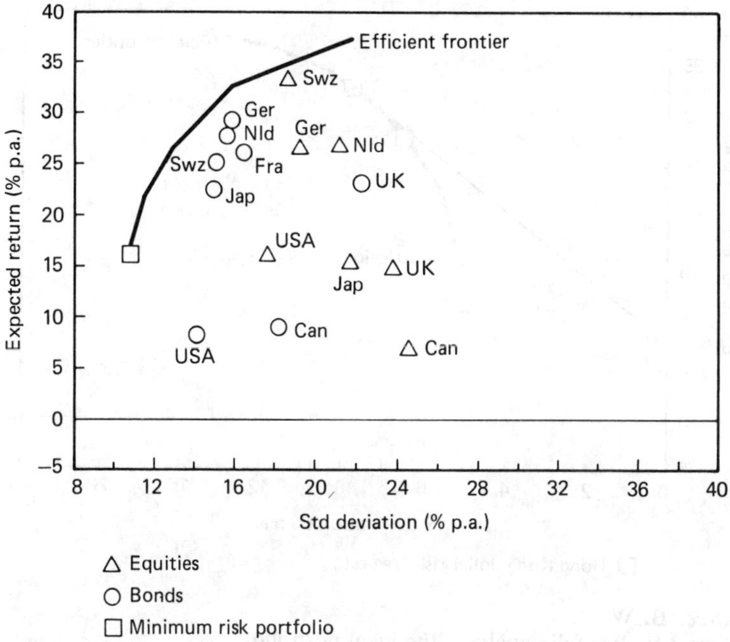

Source: BZW
Figure 3.4 Portfolio analysis: twelve-month forecasts

These sages used a mixture of alchemy and intelligence to devise the asset allocation for their clients. We have moved on. We have a forecasting group, which meets monthly to crystallise its views on the markets into quantified forecasts on a three – and twelve-month view. The three-month forecasts are used to flag the imminent direction of market movements so that any changes in asset allocation can be sensibly timed. It is the twelve-month forecasts which are used in our efficient frontier models. If we put the forecasts into the model, Figure 3.4 emerges. Remembering the objectives of low risk and a minimum of 60 per cent in equities, where on the 'frontier' in Figure 3.4 is the most appropriate portfolio?

There are two ways of establishing the point on the efficient frontier that represents the ideal portfolio. Referring to Figure 3.5 the first method is by calculation of the optimal point by reference to the gradient, which gives us Portfolio *A*. The second method is by setting a tangent from cash, Portfolio *B*. What is not possible, is to set an absolute level of risk (volatility) and always choose that point. It

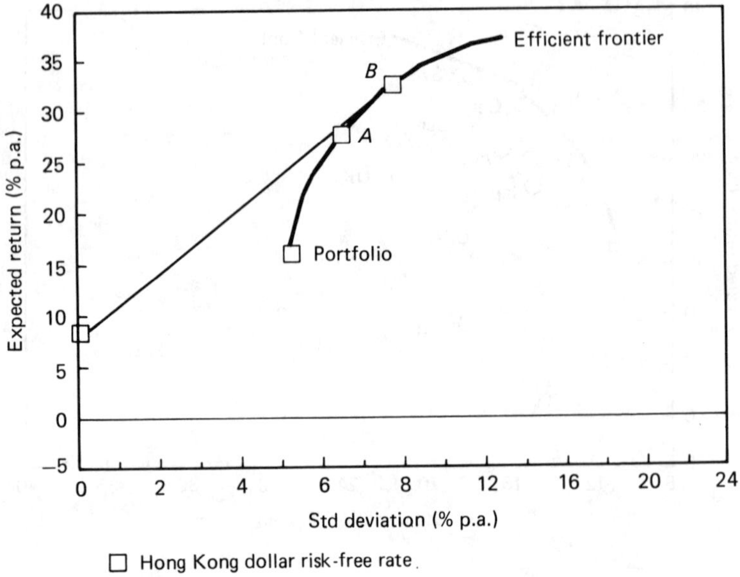

Source: BZW
Figure 3.5 Portfolio analysis: the ideal portfolio

has to be a subjective decision. The radically different shapes of the efficient frontier in Figure 3.6 which were both drawn for the same client but at different times and therefore with different forecasts, illustrate the point.

Once we have chosen the optimal position on the frontier, we would then screen the resulting asset allocation, taking note of:

- The peer group asset allocation.
- The ease and cost of dealing in the markets concerned.
- The reliability of the data.

For example, although risk data exists for Finland and Austria, these markets have changed markedly in the recent past, becoming more 'efficient'. They appear to have low volatility but this is no longer reliable.

Spain is perhaps a more interesting example. For years it appeared to be a very low volatility market. But scrutiny of performance revealed that the steady trend had been one way – downwards. The Spanish market may have been a useful tool to reduce volatility, but it certainly would not have helped performance.

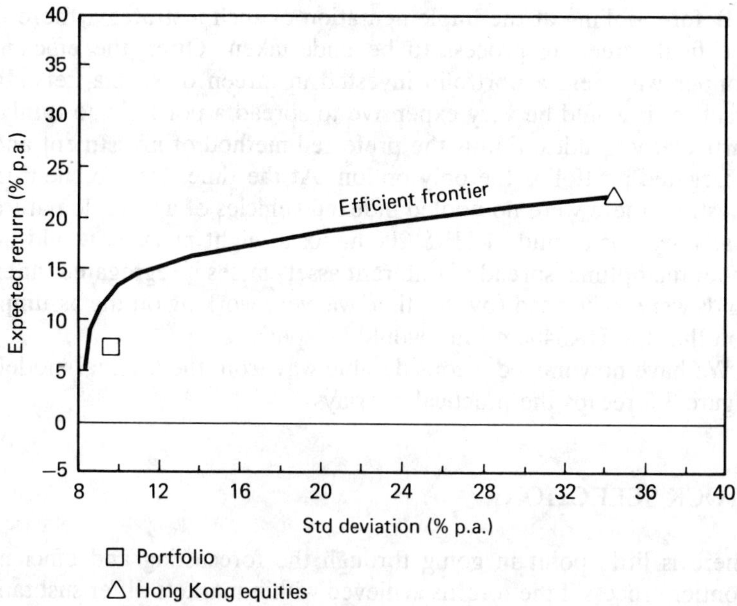

Source: BZW
Figure 3.6 Portfolio analysis: 31 December 1987

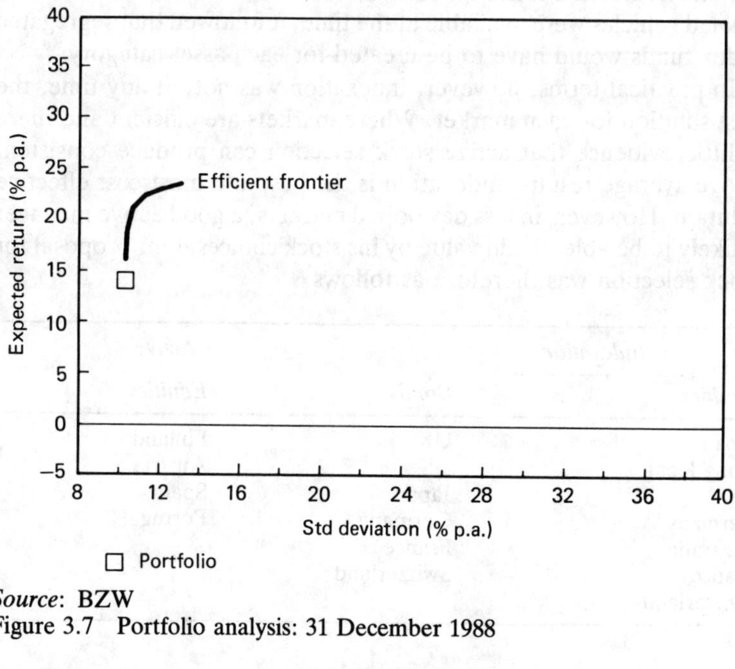

Source: BZW
Figure 3.7 Portfolio analysis: 31 December 1988

Before looking at the implementation of such a strategy, there is one final screening process to be undertaken. Often the efficient frontier will yield a portfolio invested in fifteen or so markets. In practice, it would be very expensive to spread a portfolio so thinly, particularly if indexation is the preferred method of investment and segregated portfolios the only option. At the time, for the client in question, there were no pooled indexed vehicles of a suitable nature available. For a fund of HK$ 200m, six to eight markets would be about the optimal spread of different asset classes if segregated index funds were to be used (by this time we were working on the assumption that the HK$400m fund would be split).

We have now moved a considerable way from the original model. Figure 3.8 recaps the practical overlays.

STOCK SELECTION

There is little point in going through the forecasting and efficient frontier process if the returns achieved within markets differ susbtantially from the predictions. Always assuming, of course, that the predictions are accurate! The logical solution is to use indexation as the stock selection technique to minimise stock selection risk. As no pooled vehicles were available at the time, it followed that segregated index funds would have to be created for each asset category.

In practical terms, however, indexation was not, at any time, the best solution for each market. Where markets are efficient and there is little evidence that active stock selection can produce consistent above average results, indexation is the best and most cost effective solution. However, in less developed markets, a good active manager is likely to be able to add value by his stock choices. Our proposal for stock selection was therefore as follows.

Indexation		*Active*
Equities	*Bonds*	*Equities*
Japan	UK	Finland
Hong Kong	US	Austria
UK	Japan	Spain
Germany	Germany	Portugal
Australia	France	
France	Switzerland	
Switzerland		

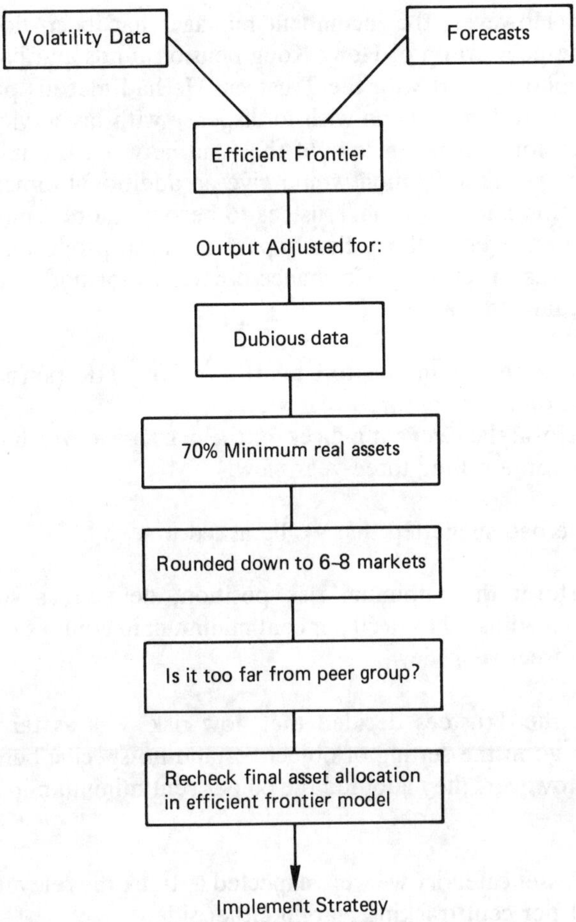

Source: BZW
Figure 3.8 Portfolio analysis: strategy flow chart

This was the view in 1985. Now we would be able to create index funds in all these markets.

As this paper is not about the practicalities of indexation, this is not the place to discuss the merits of the various construction methods. Suffice to say that we now had a complete proposal to make to the prospective Hong Kong client. All that remained was to convince the Trustees of the merits of our recommendations. The proposal received a warm welcome as a disciplined approach to solving their problems. However, the incumbent manager had been doing well against the peer group of Hong Kong pension funds and had established a good rapport with the Trustees. He had met his particular objectives and there was no wish to dispense with his services.

The decision was taken to split the fund between the incumbent and ourselves. This solution would give an additional dimension of diversification and allow the Trustees to become more familiar with what was perceived as the radical departure of our proposal. All that remained was to set the performance objectives for both managers.

The incumbent was asked to:

- Produce a return in the top quartile of the HK pension fund universe on a rolling three-year view.
- Out-perform the relevant indices for the markets in which he chose to invest on a rolling three-year view.

Initially we had suggested that we be asked to:

- Out-perform the minimum risk position, defined as shown in Figure 3.3 adjusted for a 60 per cent minimum in equities rule, on a rolling three- year view.

However, the Trustees decided that 'low risk' was as far as they wanted to go in the setting of objectives and no specific benchmark was set. However, they adopted the 60 per cent minimum in equities rule.

- In each asset category we were expected to track the relevant index with a 1 per cent tracking margin either side.

This wide tracking margin was agreed because segregated index funds were the only option, and in the case of some markets the amount invested would be small. The Trustees understood that in the case of certain markets we would be using our skills to try to out-perform, but they wanted to limit the stock selection risk in this way. The agreements were signed, the start date was fixed and we went back to London to start work.

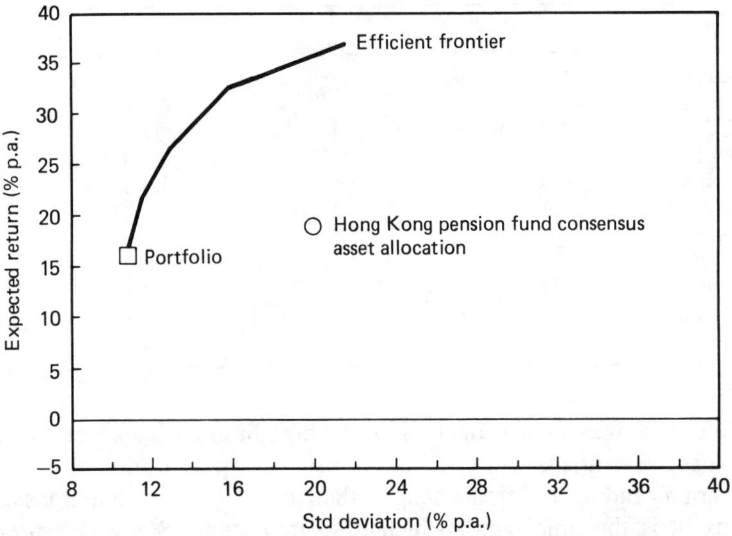

Source: BZW

Figure 3.9 Portfolio analysis: minimising the cost of reorganisation

MANAGING THE PORTFOLIO

At this stage we were nervous. It is only natural to compare results from two managers managing part of the same scheme. Did the Trustees really understand the vital difference between the two portfolios? Would they remember that our portfolio was supposed to be low risk and was likely to have a very different performance from that of other Hong Kong funds? Only time would tell.

Meanwhile, part of our brief had been to minimise the cost of reorganisation.

We ran the efficient frontier, and we got Figure 3.9.

The Trustees had asked the existing managers to liquidate half their portfolio, so the transfer to us was going to be in cash. The average Hong Kong pension's asset allocation is shown as a circle in Figure 3.9, along with the efficient frontier and the minimum risk portfolio which is where we decided to structure the fund in the first instance. The minimum risk portfolio was as follows.

Asset category	*(%)*
Equities	
Hong Kong	7.6
US	17.3
German	12.4
Swiss	10.9
Japanese	12.2
Bonds	
US	4.7
Swiss	3.3
Japanese	11.8
Liquidity	19.8

We then drew up lists of stocks to be bought in each market. Once the lists were finalised we decided to use a program trade. Although program trading is often cheaper than dealing individual transactions, it is the time factor which is so important. Being measured against the indices from day one, we could not take the time risk of delaying the creation of the portfolio. If the markets moved whilst the index funds were in the process of being constructed, we would be likely to incur substantial tracking error. It was therefore far preferable to create the portfolios in one large trade.

The secret of program trading is in accurate descriptions. The chances of successfully using this method twice would be seriously diminished if the market maker feels he has been given misleading information. It is also the case that past accuracy leads to finer terms in the future.

Each of three leading international market makers were asked to quote for the business. They did this in the form of offer prices around the mid-market prices at close of business that day for each of the markets concerned. The most competitive quote was identified and just before the close of business for each of the markets involved, we released the stock lists. The portfolio was reconstructed at a stroke. The total cost of the exercise worked out at only some 0.4 per cent of the total value of the portfolio, not including non-negotiable costs such as taxes.

Each quarter we produced detailed reports of our activities on behalf of the portfolio to discuss with the Trustees. Given that our asset allocation tended to have a significantly lower percentage in Hong Kong equities than that of the peer group, the performance of our portion of the fund was quite different to the performance achieved by the incumbent manager. But, as we were deliberately running a low risk portfolio, the Trustees *expected* us to achieve a lower, but less volatile, return.

Then came the crash of 1987. The low risk strategy made our fund a star performer. Indeed, the volatility of the Hong Kong market during the recent Chinese troubles has meant that, since inception, the low risk portfolio has performed better than the traditionally managed fund. The Trustees are pleased that both parts of the portfolio are meeting their objectives and that the sum of the two parts has had the unexpected effect of making theirs one of the best performing Hong Kong funds. Not quite the point, but a good one on which to end this case study.

4 A Non-linear Model of Portfolio Behaviour With Time-varying Expectations and Risks

David Blake

INTRODUCTION

There are now many examples of empirical single-period mean-variance (*mv*) models of portfolio behaviour.[1] The main features of these models are that:

1. the *mv* utility functions underlying their optimising behaviour have marginal rates of substitution between *m* and *v* that are independent of asset holdings; this leads to linear asset demand systems with the optimal holdings of assets determined explicitly;
2. the estimates of the expectations and risks of the returns on the assets in the portfolios are generally backward-looking, often determined as constants or moving averages from the historical sample;
3. little attention is generally paid to the question of the dynamic adjustment of the portfolio; this implicitly assumes that individuals are always, or are at least quite close to, holding optimal portfolios.

Aivazian *et al.* (1983) have attempted to generalise the traditional *mv* utility functions by using flexible functional forms. This has the effect of making the optimal demands for assets non-linear, and so implicit rather than explicit. This is because, with this type of functional form, the MRS between *m* and *v* is no longer independent of asset holdings.

In this paper, we attempt to deal with the second two features in a slightly more general way. We propose a model for asset return expectations and risks which is dynamic and forward-looking, and we deal with the question of dynamic adjustment in a more formal manner. We also pay some attention to the structure of *mv* utility functions, but in a different way to that of Aivazian *et al.* (1983).

The organisation of the paper is as follows. In the second section, we derive a general *mv* model of portfolio behaviour that is based on stochastic processes that are discrete-time analogues of Ito processes. However, the general model is not operational because it depends on the portfolio holder's preferences and assessments of portfolio characteristics, namely expectations and risks,[2] that are not observable to the investigator; further, it is a static model of behaviour. The next three sections give a structure to the individual's preferences, his expectations and risks and the dynamic adjustment of his portfolio. The sixth section considers estimation problems. Finally in the seventh section we consider some preliminary evidence for the model based on the portfolios of UK private sector pension funds.

THE MODEL OF PORTFOLIO BEHAVIOUR

Asset Price, Inflation and Exchange Rate Dynamics

We will suppose that the nominal rate of change of price of the ith asset (P_{it}) is given by the stochastic process

$$\Pi_{it} \equiv \frac{P_{it} - P_{i,\,t-1}}{P_{i,\,t-1}} = \mu_{it} + \sigma_{it}\zeta_{it} \qquad i = 1, N \tag{4.1}$$

which is the sum of a deterministic but time-varying expected rate of price change μ_{it}, and a stochastic process comprising the product of σ_{it} (a deterministic but time-varying standard deviation of price) and ζ_{it} (a standard normal stochastic variable). Equations of the form (4.1) are discrete-time analogues of Ito processes (see, e.g., Merton, 1969; 1971).[3]

Suppose in addition that inflation is given by the stochastic process (where P_t is the price level)

$$\pi_t \equiv \frac{P_t - P_{t-1}}{P_{t-1}} = \mu_{\pi t} + \sigma_{\pi t}\zeta_{\pi t} \tag{4.2}$$

with mean $\mu_{\pi t}$ and standard deviation $\sigma_{\pi t}$, and that the exchange rate change is given by the stochastic process (where e_t is the exchange rate)

$$\pi_{et} \equiv \frac{e_t - e_{t-1}}{e_{t-1}} = \mu_{et} + \sigma_{et}\zeta_{et} \tag{4.3}$$

with mean μ_{et} and standard deviation σ_{et}.

We know that functions of discrete-time stochastic processes can be differentiated using the discrete-time version of Ito's Lemma; see, e.g., Chow (1979). So, for example, the real rate of change of the price of (capital gain on) the ith asset is (where $p_{it} \equiv P_{it}/P_t$)

$$\begin{aligned} \pi_{it} &\equiv \frac{p_{it} - p_{i,\,t-1}}{p_{i,\,t-1}} \\ &= \frac{\Delta p_{it}}{p_{i,\,t-1}} - \frac{\Delta p_t}{p_{t-1}} - \left(\frac{\Delta p_{it}}{p_{i,\,t-1}}\right)\left(\frac{\Delta p_t}{p_{t-1}}\right) + \left(\frac{\Delta p_t}{p_{t-1}}\right)^2 \\ &= (\mu_{it} - \mu_{\pi t} - \sigma_{i\pi t} + \sigma^2_{\pi t}) + (\sigma_{it}\zeta_{it} - \sigma_{\pi t}\zeta_{\pi t}) \\ &= \rho_{it} + \varepsilon_{it} \qquad i = 1, N' \end{aligned} \tag{4.4}$$

since the third and fourth terms on the second line of equation (4.4) are respectively the covariance between the price of the ith asset and inflation and the variance of inflation; see, e.g., Fischer (1975).

If an asset is held overseas, with the nominal price there given by $P_i^{\$}$, the real price in terms of domestic currency is $p_i \equiv P_i^{\$}/eP$ (with the exchange rate defined as foreign currency in units of domestic currency, e.g., \$ per £). The corresponding real rate of capital gain is

$$\begin{aligned} \pi_{it} &= (\mu_{it} - \mu_{\pi t} - \mu_{et} - \sigma_{i\pi t} - \sigma_{iet} + \sigma_{e\pi t} + \sigma^2_{\pi t} + \sigma^2_{et}) \\ &\quad + (\sigma_{it}\zeta_{it} - \sigma_{\pi t}\zeta_{\pi t} - \sigma_{et}\zeta_{et}) \\ &= \rho_{it} + \varepsilon_{it} \qquad i = N' + 1, N \end{aligned} \tag{4.5}$$

For the riskless asset (in nominal terms at least)

$$\begin{aligned} \pi_{ot} &= (-\mu_{\pi t} + \sigma^2_{\pi t}) - \sigma_{\pi t}\zeta_{\pi t} \\ &= \rho_{ot} + \varepsilon_{ot} \end{aligned} \tag{4.6}$$

with a negative expected real rate of change unless the variance of inflation is sufficiently large. The variance of the real return on the riskless asset is equal to the variance of inflation.

Budget and Wealth Constraints

We make the following additional definitions:

$x_{i,\,t-1}$	real value of asset i held at the end of time period $t-1$, where $i = 0$ corresponds to the riskless asset, $i = 1, N'$ corresponds to the risky domestic assets and $i = N' + 1, N$ corresponds to the risky overseas assets
R_{it}	nominal rate of return (interest, dividend or rental) earned on asset i during t; assumed to be non-stochastic
d_{it}	net demand for asset i during t
y_t	total real non-asset income during t
c_t	real consumption during t
w_{t-1}	total real wealth at the end of $t-1$

The real wealth or balance sheet constraint at the beginning of period t (end of $t-1$) is given by

$$w_{t-1} = x_{0,\,t-1} + \sum_{i=1}^{N} x_{i,\,t-1} \tag{4.7}$$

The real budget constraint during period t is

$$\sum_{i=1}^{N} d_{it} = y_t - c_t \tag{4.8}$$

The change in total wealth during period t (the wealth accumulation equation) is

$$\Delta w_t = \sum_{i=0}^{N} \pi_{it}^{o} x_{it}^{*} \tag{4.9}$$

defining $\pi_{it}^{o} \equiv \pi_{it} + R_{it}$ as real capital gains plus nominal interest and $x_{it}^{*} \equiv x_{i,\,t-1} + d_{it}$ as existing holdings plus net acquisitions.

The level of real wealth at the end of t is given by $w_t = w_{t-1} + \Delta w_t$. We will find it convenient to use equations (4.7) and (4.8) to eliminate the holdings of the riskless asset from this. Thus we have

$$w_t = (1 + \pi_{ot}^{o}) w_t^{*} + \sum_{i=1}^{N} \pi_{it}^{*} x_{it}^{*} \tag{4.10}$$

where $\pi^*_{it} = \pi^o_{it} - \pi^o_{ot}$ is the total real rate of return on the ith risky financial asset *in excess of* that on the riskless asset (i.e., the risk premium) and where $w^*_t = w_{t-1} + y_t - c_t$ is beginning of period wealth plus (non-asset) savings.

The expected value at the beginning of t (end of $t-1$) of wealth at the end of t is given by

$$\begin{aligned} m_t &= E_{t-1}(w_t) \\ &= (1 + \rho^o_{ot})w^*_t + \sum_{i=1}^{N} \rho^*_{it}x^*_{it} \\ &= (1 + \rho^o_{ot})w^*_t + (\boldsymbol{\rho}^*_t)'(\boldsymbol{x}^*_t) \end{aligned} \tag{4.11}$$

where $\rho^o_{ot} = (R_{ot} - \mu_{\pi t} + \sigma^2_{\pi t})$ and ρ^*_{it} equals $(\mu_{it} - \sigma_{i\pi t} + R_{it} - R_{ot})$ or $(\mu_{it} - \mu_{et} - \sigma_{i\pi t} - \sigma_{iet} + \sigma^2_{e\pi t} + \sigma_{\varepsilon\tau} + R_{it} - R_{ot})$ depending on whether the asset is held at home or abroad.

The variance of wealth is given by

$$\begin{aligned} v_t &= E_{t-1}(w_t - m_t)^2 \\ &= E_{t-1}\left((-\sigma_{\pi t}\zeta_{\pi t})w^*_t + \sum_{i=1}^{N'} (\sigma_{it}\zeta_{it})x^*_{it} + \right. \\ &\quad \left. + \sum_{i=N'+1}^{N} (\sigma_{it}\zeta_{it} - \sigma_{et}\zeta_{et})x^*_{it} \right)^2 \\ &= \sigma^2_{\pi t}(w^*_t)^2 + 2(\boldsymbol{\zeta}'_t\, \boldsymbol{x}^*_t)w^*_t + (\boldsymbol{x}^*_t)'\, \boldsymbol{\Gamma}_t\, \boldsymbol{x}^*_t \\ &= (w^*_t : \boldsymbol{x}^*_t)'\, \Gamma^x_t\, (w^*_t : \boldsymbol{x}^*_t) \end{aligned} \tag{4.12}$$

where

$$\Gamma^x_t = \left[\begin{array}{c:c} \sigma^2_{\pi t} & \boldsymbol{\xi}'_t \\ \hdashline \boldsymbol{\xi}_t & \Gamma_t \end{array} \right] \tag{4.13}$$

Equation (4.11) implies that the expected value of the portfolio at the end of t, conditional on information at the beginning of t, depends on w^*_t, the total value of the portfolio at the beginning of t; $\boldsymbol{x}^*_t$, the total holdings of risky assets at the beginning of t; ρ^o_{ot}, the expected real return on the riskless asset; and $\boldsymbol{\rho}^*_t$, the expected excess returns on the risky assets during t. Equation (4.12) implies that the variance of the portfolio at the end of t, conditional on information at the beginning of t, depends on $\sigma^2_{\pi t}$, the variance of the inflation rate during t, $\boldsymbol{\xi}_t$ the covariances between the risky assets' real returns and inflation during t, and Γ_t, the covariances between the real returns on the risky assets during t. We interpret m_t and v_t as the dynamic forward-looking portfolio characteristics, expectations and risks.

The Optimal Consumption–Portfolio Strategy

The individual's objective is assumed to be

$$\max_{c_t,\, \boldsymbol{x}^*_t} \bar{u}(c_t) + u(m_t, v_t \mid w^*_t) \tag{4.14}$$

This can be done unrestrictedly since the budget and wealth constraints have already been incorporated in the definitions of m_t and v_t. Equation (4.14) reflects the idea that, at any time t, utility depends on the current level of consumption, c_t, and the assessed characteristics of the portfolio, m_t and v_t which, in turn, represent the individual's attitude, expressed in terms of expectations and risks, to the future consumption potential embodied in the portfolio at t.[4] The first-order conditions for a maximum are

$$\bar{u}_c = (1 + \rho^o_{ot})u_m \tag{4.15}$$

and

$$\mu_m \rho^*_{it} + 2u_v \left(\xi_{it} w^*_t + \sum_{j=1}^{N} \gamma_{ijt}\, x^*_{jt} \right) = 0 \qquad i = 1,N$$

or

$$\boldsymbol{\rho}^*_t + 2\frac{u_v}{u_m} (\boldsymbol{\xi}_t w^*_t + \Gamma_t \boldsymbol{x}^*_t) = 0 \tag{4.16}$$

Equation (4.15) is the conventional intertemporal envelope condition for optimal consumption and the latter is found by inverting the LHS of (4.15). Equation (4.16) gives the optimal demands for assets. In general, no explicit solution for $\boldsymbol{x}^*_t$ exists. This follows because in general

$$\psi(m_t, v_t \mid w^*_t) = 2\,\frac{u_v}{u_m} \tag{4.17}$$

is a function of m_t and v_t which also depend on $\boldsymbol{x}_t^*$. This is quite typical of demand systems as a whole. Only in the special case where the marginal rate of substitution between characteristics is independent of asset holdings so that

$$\psi = \psi(w_t^*) \tag{4.18}$$

does an explicit solution to equation (4.16) exist, namely

$$\boldsymbol{x}_t^* = -\Gamma_t^{-1}\,(\psi(w_t^*)^{-1}\boldsymbol{\rho}_t^* + \boldsymbol{\xi}_t\, w_t^*) \tag{4.19}$$

As it stands, equation (4.16) is not an operational demand system, because we do not observe the individual's attitude to risk, nor his measurements of expectations or risks; it is also a static or long-run equilibrium model of portfolio behaviour. In order to make the model operational, we must (1) model the individual's preferences, (2) model the individual's asset return expectations and risks generation processes, and (3) model the dynamic adjustment of the portfolio. These topics are discussed in the next three sections and estimation problems are then considered.

MODELLING PREFERENCES OVER EXPECTATIONS AND RISKS

In equation (4.17), ψ is twice the marginal rate of substitution between m_t and v_t. In general ψ will depend on m_t and v_t, possibly in some non-linear manner such as

$$\psi = -\alpha\left(\frac{v_t}{m_t}\right)^{\beta} \tag{4.20}$$

so that demands for assets, while depending on the means and variances of the assets separately, also depend on the mean and variance of the portfolio taken as a whole.

Equation (4.20) is consistent with the constant elasticity of substitution (CES) utility function

$$u(m_t, v_t) = \left(\delta_1 m_t^{-\delta_3} - \frac{\delta_2}{2}\, v_t^{-\delta_3}\right)^{-1/\delta_3} \tag{4.21}$$

Economic theory requires $\delta_1 > 0$, $\delta_2 > 0$, and $\delta_3 \geqslant -1$. The CES utility function has a constant elasticity of substitution between m_t and v_t of $\sigma_{mv} = (1 + \delta_3)^{-1}$ and a marginal rate of substitution between m_t and v_t of

$$\psi = -\frac{\delta_2}{\delta_1}\left(\frac{v_t}{m_t}\right)^{-(1+\delta_3)} \tag{4.22}$$

A special case of this is the Cobb–Douglas (CD) utility function which has a constant elasticity of unity (i.e. $\delta_3 = 0$).

It is important to note, however that, while the elasticity of substitution (though not the marginal rate of substitution) between m and v is constant for both utility functions, this does not imply that the elasticity of substitution between the assets in the portfolio is constant. This latter result would be somewhat unsatisfactory, since it would imply constant portfolio shares for the assets, regardless of expected returns and variances, etc. The non-constancy of substitution between assets follows because, while m_t is homogeneous of degree one in w_t^* and x_t^*, v_t is homogeneous of degree two, so that $u(m_t, v_t|w_t^*)$ is not homogeneous.

Equation (4.20) is not the only nor even the most general functional form for modelling mv utility functions.[5] But it is one of the simplest ways of introducing a MRS between m_t and v_t which is not independent of asset holdings.

MODELLING EXPECTATIONS AND RISKS

The Choice of Indicators of Asset Characteristics

Portfolio behaviour has two important components: portfolio selection and asset price forecasting. Individual optimal portfolio selection is given by equation (4.16): it implicitly solves optimal asset demands conditional on individual preferences $(2u_v/u_m)$, expectations $(\boldsymbol{\rho}_t^*)$, risks $(\sigma^2_{\pi t}, \boldsymbol{\xi}_t$ and $\Gamma_t)$ and wealth (w_t^*). Equation (4.16) will in general differ for different individuals. Asset price forecasting is the other important component of portfolio behaviour because it is from these equations that the asset characteristics, expectations and risks, are derived.

In theory, equilibrium asset prices are found by aggregating the asset demands implicit in equation (4.16) over all individuals, equating to asset supplies and solving for prices. Similarly, asset price forecasts can be derived from expected demands and supplies. However, this requires information on individual preferences, expectations, risks and wealth, all of which are in general unobservable. This procedure does not therefore provide, in general, a practical method for deriving an asset price forecasting model.

In this section, we propose an alternative forecasting model which depends only on information which is observable to all asset market participants. We begin with the recognition that, while individual asset demands may not be observable, the market outcome, namely asset prices themselves, are observable. Further, we note that asset prices appear to respond to information that is also observable. We will call these pieces of information to which asset prices respond 'characteristic indicator variables', because the asset characteristics ultimately depend on them.

Suppose that the forecasting model for real domestically-denominated asset returns depends on the following linear reduced form system for asset prices:

$$\pi^o_{ot} = \boldsymbol{a}_o' \, z_{t-1} + \varepsilon_{ot} \tag{4.23}$$

and

$$\boldsymbol{\pi}^*_t = A \, z_{t-1} + \boldsymbol{\varepsilon}_t \tag{4.24}$$

The z_{t-1} are ℓ characteristic indicator variables. The $\boldsymbol{a}_o$ and A parameters relate the z_{t-1} to the real returns and ε_{ot} and $\boldsymbol{\varepsilon}_t$ are stochastic errors involved in this relationship.[6] Because the forecasts are one period ahead, the zs must be dated $t-1$ or earlier. This is consistent with that used elsewhere (e.g., Ferson, 1983; and Gibbons and Ferson, 1985).

We will assume that the most important indicator variables are macroeconomic variables. This is because it is generally macroeconomic information which has the greatest impact on asset price movements as a whole. Microeconomic (i.e., firm- or industry-specific) information will certainly have an influence on the movement of individual asset prices, but in an aggregate model, it is impossible to capture all the microeconomic variables which influence price movements at home and overseas. It is possible that the form in which these variables appear is also of importance. We postulate two different forms for the indicators, designated 'exogenous indicators' and 'cyclical indicators'. Models with exogenous indicators have been estimated by Fama (1981), for example. Models with cyclical indicators are motivated by the observed correlation between asset prices and aggregate economic activity over the business cycle that has been recognised at least since Burns and Mitchell (1956).

Modelling the Expectations and Risks Characteristics

Expectations and risks are based on the asset price forecasting equations (4.23) and (4.24). We consider several possible formulations.

Rational Expectations[7]

With rational expectations, the problems of determining the expected values and variances of real returns are intimately linked and both solutions fall out naturally from the model generating asset returns. Given equations (4.23) and (4.24), then conditional on all the information available at time $t - 1$, the full-information rational expectation of asset returns are

$$E_{t-1}(\pi_{ot}^{o}) \equiv \rho_{ot}^{o} = \boldsymbol{a}_o' \, z_{t-1} \tag{4.25}$$

and

$$E_{t-1}(\boldsymbol{\pi}_t^{*}) \equiv \boldsymbol{\rho}_t^{*} = A \, z_{t-1} \tag{4.26}$$

With this model, expected returns are time-varying; see Gibbons and Ferson (1985) for an example of a model with time-varying expected returns. The variance components are derived from the unanticipated components of equations (4.23) and (4.24) but are assumed to be time-invariant

$$\text{var}\begin{bmatrix} \pi_{ot}^{o} \\ \hline \boldsymbol{\pi}_t^{*} \end{bmatrix} = E\left[\begin{array}{c|c} \varepsilon_{ot}^2 & \varepsilon_{ot}\boldsymbol{\varepsilon}_t' \\ \hline \boldsymbol{\varepsilon}_t\varepsilon_{ot} & \boldsymbol{\varepsilon}_t\boldsymbol{\varepsilon}_t' \end{array}\right] = \left[\begin{array}{c|c} \sigma_\pi^2 & \boldsymbol{\xi}' \\ \hline \boldsymbol{\xi} & \Gamma \end{array}\right] = \Gamma^x \tag{4.27}$$

Rational Expectations With Common Dynamic Risks

The above model of expectations generation is the simplest possible rational expectations model. It is a model with dynamic means and constant variances, i.e., it assumed that the expected returns could change over time but that the risks were constant. This, of course, constitutes a fairly strong restriction and one which may be rejected by the data (see e.g., Officer, 1971; Fama, 1976, pp. 14–17; Bollerslev *et al.*, 1988). An immediately obvious modification is to allow the risks involved in portfolio decision making as well as the means to be dynamic.[8] The simplest way of doing this is to allow all the variance components to be subject to the same common dynamic effects.

Again assume that the expected returns are given by the time-varying equations (4.25) and (4.26). Now, however, suppose that the risks in asset returns are not time-invariant as in (4.27) but are time-dependent of the form

$$\mathrm{Var}\begin{bmatrix} \pi^{o}_{ot} \\ \hdashline \boldsymbol{\pi}^{*}_{t} \end{bmatrix} = \Gamma^{x}_{t}$$

$$= \sigma^2_t \Gamma^x \tag{4.28}$$

where σ^2_t is the common dynamic risk component, a positive scalar quantity and Γ^x is a positive definite matrix with time-invariant elements.

Certain obvious possibilities suggest themselves for σ^2_t:

$$\sigma^2_t = (\boldsymbol{b}' z_{t-1})^2 > 0 \tag{4.29}$$

and

$$\sigma^2_t = \exp(2\boldsymbol{b}' z_{t-1}) > 0 \tag{4.30}$$

where z_{t-1} are lagged values of macroeconomic variables appropriate for explaining the risks in the economy. The intercept of $\boldsymbol{b}'\, z_{t-1}$ is normalised on unity in (4.29) and zero in (4.30).

A number of studies have considered what factors might determine dynamic risks. For example, Grossman and Shiller (1981) consider whether they can be attributed to uncertainty concerning discount factors (i.e., the real interest rates at which dividend payments, etc. are discounted) which are, in turn, related to levels of economic activity. Alternatively Breeden (1979) and LeRoy and LaCivita (1981) have argued that consumption variability may induce asset price variability, the magnitude of which depends on the degree of risk aversion. Tobin (n.d.) considers inflation and exchange rate uncertainty.

There are, of course, other ways of modelling time-dependent risks. For example, Bollerslev *et al.* (1988) allow Γ_t^x to follow a generalised autoregressive conditional heteroscedasticity (GARCH) process. This assumes that individuals update their estimates of the means and covariances of asset returns each period using the prediction errors in last period's returns. Therefore, individuals learn about changes in Γ_t^x from information only about market returns. But in equations (4.29) and (4.30), z_{t-1} can include more general information than simply that on market returns.

Rational Expectations With Specific Dynamic Risks

This is an even more general expectations generation mechanism than the last one since it allows each element of the covariance matrix of returns to be independently (i.e., specifically) time-varying. In equation (4.28) we assumed that each element of a constant time-invariant variance–covariance matrix Γ^x is modified by the same dynamic risk factor. This means that an increase in risk will have precisely the same effect on each element of Γ^x. However, if, instead of assuming that the variances and covariances of the asset returns are constant, we assume that the correlations between assets returns are constant, then this will allow us to have an expectations model with much more general dynamic risk elements.

We know that the variance–covariance matrix of asset returns may be decomposed as

$$\begin{aligned} \text{Var}\begin{bmatrix} \pi_{ot}^{o} \\ \text{-----} \\ \boldsymbol{\pi}_t^* \end{bmatrix} &= \Gamma_t^x \\ &= \Lambda_t R^x \Lambda_t' \end{aligned} \qquad (4.31)$$

where R^x is the constant time-invariant matrix of asset return correlations (with typical element η_{ij}) and where Λ_t is the diagonal matrix of asset return standard errors which are assumed to be time-dependent (with typical diagonal element σ_{it}).

We can model the σ_{it} in a similar way to that in which we modelled σ_t^2 in equations (4.29) or (4.30), i.e.

$$\sigma_{it} = \boldsymbol{b}_i' z_{t-1} > 0 \tag{4.32}$$

or

$$\sigma_{it} = \exp(\boldsymbol{b}_i' z_{t-1}) > 0 \tag{4.33}$$

Thus a typical element of (4.31) becomes

$$\gamma_{ijt}^x = \eta_{ij} \exp(\boldsymbol{b}_i' z_{t-1} + \boldsymbol{b}_j' z_{t-1}) > 0 \tag{4.34}$$

and the dynamic component differs as i and j vary. The intercept of $\boldsymbol{b}_i' z_{t-1}$ is normalised on unity in (4.32) and zero in (4.33).

Inferred Expectations

The rational expectations analysis above relies on the assumption that the individual believes that the appropriate model is equations (4.23) and (4.24) and that all individuals have the same expectations. This is equivalent to saying that the individual knows the entire conditional distribution of the true model, including all the conditional moments and in particular the first two. This in turn is equivalent to living in a world of *risk* but not *uncertainty*.

These are very strict assumptions. Wills (1979) has proposed an alternative approach, embodying a weaker set of assumptions, which examines the outcomes of optimising behaviour in order to infer the structure generating the expectations underlying this behaviour. He argues that 'if we observe both the factors conditioning a decision-maker's expectations and his portfolio decision, we can infer the mechanism he uses to generate his expectations and his attitude to risk' (p. 4), because 'individual beliefs about expected rates of return are attempts to forecast observed outcomes' (p. 12).

Suppose that the individual does not in fact know the complete conditional distribution but knows only the first conditional moments and then only apart from some random error

$$\rho_{ot}^o = \boldsymbol{a}_o' z_{t-1} + \nu_{ot} \tag{4.35}$$

and

$$\boldsymbol{\rho}_t^* = A z_{t-1} + \boldsymbol{v}_t \tag{4.36}$$

where the $\boldsymbol{\nu}_t$ are generated by unobserved information and are taken to be orthogonal to z_{t-1} so that the prediction errors are independent of the individual's expectations.

Suppose also that the individual's model is correct so that from equations (4.23) and (4.24)

$$\pi^o_{ot} = \rho^o_{ot} + \varepsilon_{ot} \tag{4.37}$$

and

$$\boldsymbol{\pi}^*_t = \boldsymbol{\rho}^*_t + \boldsymbol{\varepsilon}_t \tag{4.38}$$

and that the individual uses the true but unknown covariance matrix of errors (4.27) as measures of risk in determining his portfolio composition from equation (4.16). This is because the error covariance matrix implied by equations (4.37) and (4.38) is contaminated by the noise ν_{ot} and $\boldsymbol{\nu}_t$ given in equations (4.35) and (4.36).

Wills argues that these assumptions are much weaker than rational expectations. For example, rational expectations would require that the prediction errors, ε_{ot} and $\boldsymbol{\varepsilon}_t$, be uncorrelated with all predetermined variables in the model and not just with the predictions. Further, these assumptions do not imply that all individuals have the same expectations. So, for example, one individual could have different expectations and hence a different portfolio than another even if they are equally risk-averse.

MODELLING THE DYNAMIC ADJUSTMENT OF THE PORTFOLIO

Equation (4.16) is a static or long-run equilibrium model since it is assumed to hold continuously, and it also implies the actual portfolios are adjusted instantly (and, indeed, costlessly) as new optimal portfolios are indicated. In the real world, however, actual portfolios are not adjusted instantly and costlessly, and we should try to capture some of the dynamics of portfolio adjustment in a systematic manner.

Lagged Adjustment to New Equilibria

One of the most promising approaches to lagged adjustment as applied to economic behaviour has been the adjustment mechanism proposed by Phillips (1954; 1957). This has been successfully applied to the consumption function by Hendry and von Ungern Sternberg (1980) and to general systems of demand equations by Anderson and Blundell (1982; 1983; 1984).

The basic idea underlying the Phillips approach is that individuals perform two optimisation exercises. The first optimisation exercise gives them their long-run equilibrium solution, i.e. equation (4.16). The second optimisation exercise gives them their optimal adjustment procedure whenever a new portfolio equilibrium emerges. So when the optimal portfolio diverges from the actual portfolio, a dynamic adjustment mechanism will begin to operate which brings the actual portfolio into line with the optimal portfolio.

The dynamic adjustment mechanism consists of derivative, proportional and integral adjustments. The proportional adjustment controls the rate of change of the stock of assets so that a disequilibrium in the portfolio of assets will generate flow changes in the portfolio leading to net purchases or sales of assets. The derivative adjustment controls the rate of change of these asset flows so that a disequilibrium in the portfolio will in addition generate accelerations or decelerations in asset stock holdings. Finally the integral adjustment controls for the cumulative disequilibrium – that is, for the discrepancy between the new equilibrium portfolio and the cumulated adjustment away from the old portfolio. However, the integral adjustment operates only when the new equilibrium is itself dynamically changing over time. When the new equilibrium portfolio is a fixed portfolio, then the optimal adjustment to it is fully controlled by the proportional and derivative components.

The short-run dynamic adjustment which has equation (4.16) as its long-run solution is of the form:

$$\begin{aligned} &\Delta\boldsymbol{\rho}_t^* + \boldsymbol{c}_1\Delta w_t^* + \boldsymbol{C}_1\Delta\boldsymbol{x}_t^* \\ &\quad + \boldsymbol{C}_2[\boldsymbol{\rho}_{t-1}^* + \psi(m_{t-1}, v_{t-1} \mid w_{t-1}^*) \\ &\quad \times (\boldsymbol{\xi}_{t-1}\, w_{t-1}^* + \boldsymbol{\Gamma}_{t-1}\, \boldsymbol{x}_{t-1}^*)] = \mathbf{0} \qquad (4.39) \end{aligned}$$

where $\boldsymbol{c}_1$ and $\boldsymbol{C}_1$ are respectively $N \times 1$ and $N \times N$ matrices of derivative dynamic adjustment parameters and $\boldsymbol{C}_2$ is an $N \times N$ matrix of proportional dynamic adjustment parameters.

On the assumption that the new long-run equilibrium is a static equilibrium, then the full dynamic adjustment takes place exclusively through derivative and proportional elements, and there is therefore no integral dynamic adjustment component in equation (4.39). We also assume, in deriving the proportional adjustment mechanism, that changes in ψ are sufficiently small that they can be ignored. At the very minimum we should expect to have $\boldsymbol{c}_1$ full and C_1 and C_2 as diagonal matrices. Cross-asset dynamic substitution effects will arise whenever C_1 and C_2 have non-zero off-diagonal elements.

Slowly Adjusting or Highly Uncertain Expectations, Taxes and Transactions Costs

There are several reasons why we might expect slow adjustment of the portfolio. First, there may be slow adjustment of expectations so that individuals take time to realise that the world has changed. Alternatively, expectations can be highly uncertain, so that individuals are prepared to wait before they accept that the world has changed. In the model of expectations generation, equations (4.23) and (4.24), the z_{t-1} can include lagged macroeconomic variables so that expectations respond with a lag to changes in z_{t-1}. Secondly, the tax treatment of assets may either advance or retard the adjustment to the portfolio. Thirdly, there may be costs of making portfolio adjustments as a result of transactions costs. However, it is arguable that the institutional structure of brokerage commissions (i.e., decreasing costs to scale) make it unlikely that they will have much impact in delaying adjustments to the portfolio, especially for very large traders such as pension funds.

This implies, therefore that, in terms of transactions costs, once a change or an expected change in the world is perceived, then it is both optimal and efficient for individuals to move directly to their new equilibrium portfolios; so the only valid reasons for slow adjustments to the portfolio is sluggishness or caution in interpretation of expectations and delays designed to minimise the tax burden.

To incorporate all these factors fully into the portfolio model of would clearly be very complicated. What in fact we propose is to let the sluggishness of expectations be carried by the lag structure of z_t and to modify the total returns on assets for brokerage commission and taxes.

ESTIMATION

In general, the following sets of parameters have to be estimated: the parameters of the model generating the dynamic expectations and risks; the parameters determining the preferences for different asset characteristics; and the parameters determining the dynamic adjustment of the portfolio.

The model to be estimated (in the case of CES preferences) is

$$\begin{aligned} \Delta \boldsymbol{\rho}_t^* &+ \boldsymbol{c}_1 \Delta w_t^* + C_1 \Delta \boldsymbol{x}_t^* \\ &+ C_2 \left[\boldsymbol{\rho}_{t-1}^* - \left(\frac{\delta_2}{\delta_1}\right)\left(\frac{v_{t-1}}{m_{t-1}}\right)^{-(1+\delta_3)} \right. \\ &\times \left. (\boldsymbol{\xi}_{t-1} w_{t-1}^* + \Gamma_{t-1} \boldsymbol{x}_{t-1}^*) \right] = \boldsymbol{e}_t \end{aligned} \tag{4.40}$$

where $\boldsymbol{e}_t$ is a vector of estimation errors.

In ordinary demand systems, both prices and quantities are jointly endogenous. In equation (4.40) the only endogenous variables are asset quantities ($\Delta \boldsymbol{x}_t^*$). Information on prices appears only in the form of expected returns (e.g., $\Delta \boldsymbol{\rho}_t^*$) and can therefore be treated as predetermined, since the expected values are functions of predetermined variables (i.e. z_{t-1}).

While it would be more efficient to estimate equation (4.40) in a single stage, it may not be feasible if A, C_1 or C_2 are both of large dimension and dense. If A, C_1 and C_2 are large then a severe set of zero restrictions must be imposed if equation (4.40) is to be estimated in a single stage; for example, C_1 may have to be a fully diagonal matrix and blocks of off-diagonal zero restrictions may have to be imposed on C_2.

As an alternative to the single stage estimation of equation (4.40), it is possible to estimate it in two stages. At the first stage, we estimate $\boldsymbol{a}_o$ and A, the parameters of the equations generating the expectations of the total real returns on assets. These are the parameters of the individual's forecasting equations and we take the resulting forecasts (and also the resulting estimates of the risk factors) and substitute them into equation (4.40). Then at the second stage we estimate the remaining parameters of equation (4.40) (i.e., (δ_2/δ_1), δ_3, $\boldsymbol{c}_1$, C_1 and C_2) taking as given the estimates of $\boldsymbol{a}_o$ and A, etc. from the first stage. While this two-stage estimation procedure is likely to be inefficient, it is nevertheless consistent (as long as an instrumental variable estimator is used at the second stage) and has the additional advantage of allowing a model to be estimated which has a larger number of assets and which embodies a less restricted structure of dynamic adjustment. However, because $\boldsymbol{a}_o$ and A, etc. are estimates and not true population parameters, inferences using the second stage standard errors for the remaining parameters may not be strictly valid. These arguments follow from Pagan (1984), although he considered only linear models at each of the two stages.

A further point concerns that of identification. Only the ratio (δ_2/δ_1) in equation (4.40) is identified, so we cannot estimate δ_1 and δ_2 separately: but this is not a real problem because it is only the ratio and not δ_1 and δ_2 separately that is relevant for behaviour. However all the remaining parameters in equation (4.40) are identified. In particular, we should note that the relationship between (δ_2/δ_1), A, C_2, $\boldsymbol{\xi}_{t-1}$ and Γ_{t-1} leaves no problems for identification. C_2 is identified because A is identified from the term in $\Delta\boldsymbol{\rho}_t$. Also (δ_2/δ_1), $\boldsymbol{\xi}_{t-1}$ and Γ_{t-1} are identified as long as $\sigma^2_{\pi,t-1} \neq 0$ or $\delta_3 \neq 0$.

Estimating the Model Generating Expectations and Risks

In order to estimate the model generating expectations it will be convenient to transform the errors of the model in order to render them homoscedastic. This results in a constant (i.e., time-invariant) error covariance matrix and therefore standard estimation techniques may be used. We may examine each of our possible models for generating expectations in turn. But first we define

$$\boldsymbol{\pi}_t^x = A^x z_{t-1} + \boldsymbol{\varepsilon}_t^x \tag{4.41}$$

where

$$\boldsymbol{\pi}_t^x = \left[\begin{array}{c} \pi_{ot}^o \\ \hdashline \pi_t^* \end{array}\right], \quad A^x = \left[\begin{array}{c} \boldsymbol{a}_o' \\ \hdashline A \end{array}\right], \quad \boldsymbol{\varepsilon}_t^x = \left[\begin{array}{c} \varepsilon_{ot} \\ \hdashline \boldsymbol{\varepsilon}_t \end{array}\right] \tag{4.42}$$

and then assume that $\boldsymbol{\pi}_t^x$ is multivariate normally distributed

$$\boldsymbol{\pi}_t^x \sim N(A^x z_{t-1}, \Gamma_t^x) \tag{4.43}$$

where the covariance matrix Γ_t^x differs according to the particular model generating expectations.

Rational Expectations

The appropriate covariance matrix with rational expectations is the constant and untransformed residual covariance matrix of the model in equation (4.41)

$$\begin{aligned}\Gamma_t^x &= \Gamma^x \\ &= E(\boldsymbol{\pi}_t^x - A^x z_{t-1})(\boldsymbol{\pi}^x - A^x z_{t-1})' \\ &= -\sum_t^T (\boldsymbol{\pi}_t^x - A^x z_{t-1})(\boldsymbol{\pi}_t^x - A^x z_{t-1})' \end{aligned} \tag{4.44}$$

Given equation (4.44) and the non-simultaneous nature of the model in (4.41), the consistent and efficient estimator is the seemingly unrelated equations (SURE) estimator. A consistent but inefficient estimator is OLS applied to each equation of (4.41) separately.

Rational Expectations With Common Dynamic Risks

The appropriate covariance matrix when there are common dynamic risk factors is given by equation (4.28) with (4.29) or (4.30). In the case of equations (4.28) and (4.30) we define Λ_t^{-1} as the diagonal matrix with $\exp(-\,\boldsymbol{b}'z_{t-1})$ along the main diagonal and define $\boldsymbol{\zeta}_t^x = \Lambda_t^{-1}\,\boldsymbol{\varepsilon}_t^x$. By premultiplying each side of equation (4.41) by Λ_t^{-1} we arrive at a model with homoscedastic errors

$$\Lambda_t^{-1}\,\boldsymbol{\pi}_t^x = \Lambda_t^{-1}\,A^x\,z_{t-1} + \boldsymbol{\zeta}_t^x \tag{4.45}$$

The transformed errors in equation (4.45) have a constant (i.e. time-invariant) covariance matrix Γ^x. Given the non-simultaneous nature of equation (4.45), the consistent and efficient estimator is the non-linear-in-variables SURE estimator. In the absence of a known dynamic structure for $\boldsymbol{b}'z_{t-1}$, an alternative two-stage estimation procedure can be used. This will be discussed in the next subsection.

Rational Expectations With Specific Dynamic Risks

A similar model to equation (4.45) emerges in this case, except that the transformed errors have a constant covariance matrix R^x. Again, the non-linear-in-variables SURE estimator is appropriate. Again when the dynamic structure for $b_i'z_{t-1}$ is unknown, a two-stage estimation procedure is possible.

At the first stage, equation (4.41) is estimated as with simple rational expectations – that is, without taking into account the time-varying residual covariance matrix. A typical estimated equation is

$$\pi_{it}^x = (a_i^x)'z_{t-1} + \varepsilon_{it}^x \tag{4.46}$$

We then define

$$s_{it} = 0.5\ell n\,(\varepsilon_{it}^x)^2 \tag{4.47}$$

as the estimated logarithmic standard error at t of the ith equation. From the definition of $\varepsilon_{it}^x \equiv \sigma_{it}\zeta_{it}^x = \sigma_{it}\exp(\nu_{it})$, say, and using equations (4.33) and (4.47), we get the second-stage estimation equation

$$\begin{aligned} s_{it} &= 0.5\ell n\,(\sigma_{it}\exp\,(\nu_{it}))^2 \\ &= \ell n\,\sigma_{it} + \nu_{it} \\ &= b_i'\,z_{t-1} + \nu_{it} \end{aligned} \tag{4.48}$$

Exp $(b_i'\,z_{t-1})$ is the estimated specific dynamic risk factor for the ith equation. At the second stage, equation (4.45) is estimated with Λ_t^{-1} constructed using the fitted values from (4.48). A similar two-stage procedure is required when there are common dynamic risks. The main difference is that it is a single logarithmic variance that is estimated rather than N standard errors. It is suggested that the variance is constructed from a weighted average of the N individual estimated residuals, with the weights being the value shares of assets in the balance sheet. Again the caveats of Pagan (1984) apply.

Inferred Expectations

The final model of expectations generation that we examine is the inferred expectations model of Wills (1979). This model imposes a much weaker set of restrictions than the rational expectations model. In particular, it does not require all individuals to have the same expectations even though from equations (4.35) and (4.36) there may be common agreement about which variables z_{t-1} are important for determining expectations. In addition, because Wills supposes that the individuals use the true but unknown covariance matrix of the errors (4.27) as the appropriate risk factors in determining portfolio composition, this has to be estimated as a matrix of parameters at the same time as the parameters of the characteristics preference function $\psi(m_t, v_t)$ and the parameters of the dynamic adjustment $\boldsymbol{c}_1$, C_1 and C_2 are estimated. Because the inferred expectations model has to be estimated in a single stage we shall leave all considerations of estimation until the next subsection, but simply note that the expectations generation model contained in equations (4.35)–(4.38) may be estimated in a similar way to the simple rational expectations model.

Estimating the Non-Linear Model of Portfolio Behaviour

The non-linear model of portfolio behaviour in the case of CES preferences over the characteristics m and v, and with dynamic portfolio adjustments, is given by equation (4.40). We know that it is possible to estimate this in two stages or in a single stage (except for the case of inferred expectations which must be estimated in a single stage). In either case, an instrumental variable systems estimator, such as non-linear three-stage least squares (NL3LS) is recommended.

When the model is estimated in a single stage, the risk factors with the three rational expectations schemes are functions of the parameters, $\boldsymbol{a}_o$, A and $\boldsymbol{b}$. With inferred expectations, σ_π^2, $\boldsymbol{\xi}$ and Γ are not functions of any other parameters, and therefore they have to be estimated as separate parameters, subject to the restrictions of a covariance matrix, namely that of symmetry and positive definiteness. Alternatively the Cholesky factors of the symmetric, positive definite matrix can be estimated unrestrictedly. There may be other problems with estimating equation (4.40) under inferred expectations. The first is that another ½$N(N+1)$ parameters have to be estimated over and above that of, say, the simple rational expectations model. This may be prohibitive in a large model. Secondly, identification may become a more serious problem than with the simple rational expectations model. As we noted above, the model is theoretically identified as long as $\sigma_\pi^2 \neq 0$ or $\delta_3 \neq 0$. However, in practice, identification may still prove to be rather weak and, as Wills (1979) noted, we may be unable to distinguish an individual who is very risk-averse but who does not believe that the world is very uncertain (i.e., who has Γ^x low and ψ high) from an individual who believes the world is very uncertain but who is not very risk averse (Γ^x high and ψ low).

In conclusion, therefore, the only models of portfolio behaviour which it seems feasible to estimate are those in which individuals have either simple rational expectations or rational expectations with common dynamic risk factors.

CONCLUSION

The model in equation (4.40) has been tested on the portfolios of UK private sector pension funds 1963–78. Two versions were tested, one with dynamic expectations and time-invariant risks and the other with dynamic expectations and common dynamic risks. The main findings were that

1. preferences over the portfolio characteristics m and v were found to be consistent with a Cobb–Douglas utility function, i.e., $\delta_3 = 0$;
2. there was strong evidence of expectations being time-varying;
3. there was little evidence of risks being time-varying, since the constant risks version performed as well as the common dynamic risks version;
4. there was strong evidence for slow dynamic adjustment of the portfolio, since the version of the model indicating instantaneous adjustment was always inferior;
5. the model with cyclical indicators performed better than that with exogenous indicators.

For more details see Blake (1989, 1991).

Notes

1. For the UK, examples are Parkin (1970); Parkin *et al.* (1970); Ghosh and Parkin (1970); Courakis (1974; 1975; 1980); Barrett *et al.* (1975); Honohan (1980); Spencer (1981); and Keating (1985).
2. Expectations and risks are treated in this paper as portfolio characteristics along the lines proposed in the Gorman–Lancaster characteristics model of the demand for related goods (see, e.g., Gorman, 1980). For formal treatment of this model in portfolio behaviour, see Blake (1990).

3. We assume that equations of the form (4.1) have the following properties (which follow because the time period is sufficiently small): the product of two deterministic components is zero (so that, e.g., $\mu_{it}\mu_{jt} = 0$), the product of a deterministic and stochastic component is zero (so that, e.g., $\mu_{jt}\zeta_{it} = 0$) and the product of two stochastic components is deterministic and non-zero (so that, e.g., $\zeta_{it}\zeta_{jt} = \gamma_{ijt}$, a non-zero, deterministic, time-varying cross-correlation).
4. See Blake (1990) for a complete development of this idea.
5. See Aivazian, *et al.* (1983) for an alternative approach.
6. The model in equations (4.23) and (4.24) is similar to the factor or index model of which the CAPM is one member (see, e.g., Sharpe, 1985, p. 191). But it is not identical because in the factor model the errors are assumed to be contemporaneously uncorrelated whereas in (4.23) and (4.24) this is not the case.
7. We call this model and the next two models, rational expectations models; Wills (1979) uses the same nomenclature for a similar model. But this should not be confused with Muth's original version of rational expectations in which asset price expectations could be determined from the interaction of expected demands and supplies.
8. There is a growing body of literature aimed at assessing variability of the kind proposed here. As examples applied to inflation, see Foster (1978); Cukierman and Wachtel (1979); and Pagan, Hall and Trivedi (1983).

References

V. A. Aivazian, J. L. Callen, I. Krinsky and C. C. Y. Kwan (1983) 'Mean–Variance Utility Functions and the Demand for Risky Assets: An Empirical Analysis using Flexible Functional Forms', *Journal of Financial and Quantitative Analysis*, 18, 412–24.

G. J. Anderson and R. W. Blundell (1982) 'Estimation and Hypothesis Testing in Dynamic Singular Equation Systems', *Econometrica*, 50, 1559–72.

G. J. Anderson and R. W. Blundell (1983) 'Testing Restrictions in a Flexible Dynamic Demand System: An Application to Consumers Expenditure in Canada', *Review of Economic Studies*, 50 397–410.

G. J. Anderson and R. W. Blundell (1984) 'Consumer Non-Durables in the UK: A Dynamic Demand System', *Economic Journal*, 94, Supplement, 35–44 (Annual Conference of RES and AUTE, Brasenose College, Oxford, 1983).

R. J. Barrett, M. R. Gray and J. M. Parkin (1975) 'The Demand for Financial Assets by the Personal Sector of the UK Economy', in G. Renton (ed.), *Modelling the Economy*, London: Heinemann.

D. Blake (1989) 'Testing Models Generating Time-varying Asset Return Expectations and Risks: The Case of U.K. Private Sector Pension Funds', *Economic Modelling*, 6, 220–40.

D. Blake (1990) 'Portfolio Behaviour and Asset Pricing in a Characteristics Framework', *Scottish Journal of Political Economy*, forthcoming.

D. Blake (1991) 'Testing a Non-linear Model of Portfolio Behaviour with Time-varying Expectations and Risks: The Case of U.K. Private Sector Pension Funds', *Applied Financial Economics*, forthcoming.

T. P. Bollerslev, R. F. Engle and J. M. Woolridge (1988) 'A Capital Asset Pricing Model with Time-varying Covariances', *Journal of Political Economy*, 96, 116–31.

D. Breeden (1979) 'An Intertemporal Asset Pricing Model With Stochastic Consumption and Investment Opportunities', *Journal of Finance*, 7, 265–96.

A. F. Burns and W. C. Mitchell (1956) *Measuring Business Cycles*, New York: NBER.

G. Chow (1979) 'Optimal Control of Stochastic Differential Equation Systems', *Journal of Economic Dynamics and Control*, 1, 143–75.

A. S. Courakis (1974) 'Clearing Bank Asset Choice Behaviour: A Mean Variance Treatment', *Oxford Bulletin of Economics and Statistics*, 36, 173–201.

A. S. Courakis (1975) 'Testing Theories of Discount House Portfolio Selection', *Review of Economic Studies*, 62, 643–48.

A. S. Courakis (1980) 'In Search of an Explanation of Commercial Bank Short-Run Portfolio Selection', *Oxford Bulletin of Economics and Statistics*, 42, 305–35.

A. Cukierman and P. Wachtel (1979) 'Differential Inflationary Expectations and the Variability of Inflation', *American Economic Review*, 69, 595–609.

E. F. Fama (1976) *Foundations of Finance*, Oxford: Basil Blackwell.

E. F. Fama (1981) 'Stock Returns, Real Activity, Inflation and Money', *American Economic Review*, 71, 545–65.

W. E. Ferson (1983) 'Expectations of Real Interest Rates and Aggregate Consumption: Empirical Tests', *Journal of Financial and Quantitative Analysis*, 18, 477–95.

S. Fischer (1975) 'The Demand for Index Bonds', *Journal of Political Economy*, 83, 509–34.

E. Foster (1978) 'The Variability of Inflation', *Review of Economics and Statistics*, 60, 346–50.

D. Ghosh and M. J. Parkin (1970) 'An Econometric Investigation of the Portfolio and Debt Behaviour of Building Societies', University of Essex discussion paper, 24 (June).

M. R. Gibbons and W. E. Ferson (1985) 'Testing Asset Pricing Models with Changing Expectations and an Unobservable Market Portfolio', *Journal of Financial Economics*, 14, 217–36.

W. M. Gorman (1980) 'A Possible Procedure for Analysing Quality Differentials in the Egg Market', *Review of Economic Studies*, 47, 843–56 (originally Journal Paper J–3129 of Iowa State College of Agriculture and Mechanical Arts, 1956).

S. Grossman and R. J. Shiller (1981) 'The Determinants of the Variability of Stock Market Prices', *American Economic Review*, 71, 222–9.

D. F. Hendry and T. von Ungern Sternberg (1980) 'Liquidity and Inflation

Effects on Consumers' Expenditure', in A. S. Deaton (ed.), *Essays in the Theory of Measurement of Consumer Behaviour*, Cambridge: Cambridge University Press.

P. Honohan (1980) 'Testing a Standard Theory of Portfolio Selection', *Oxford Bulletin of Economics and Statistics*, 42, 17–34.

G. Keating (1985) 'The Financial Sector of the LBS Model', in D. A. Currie (ed.), *Advances in Monetary Theory*, London: Croom Helm.

S. LeRoy and C. J. LaCivita (1981) 'Risk Aversion and the Dispersion of Asset Prices', *Journal of Business*, 54, 535–48.

R. Merton (1969) 'Lifetime Portfolio Selection Under Uncertainty: The Continuous Time Case', *Review of Economics and Statistics*, 51, 247–57.

R. Merton (1971) 'Optimal Consumption and Portfolio Rules in a Continuous Time Model', *Journal of Economic Theory*, 3, 373–413.

R. R. Officer (1971) 'A Time Series Examination of the Market Factor of the New York Stock Exchange', Ph.D. dissertation, University of Chicago.

A. Pagan (1984) 'Econometric Issues in the Analysis of Regressions with Generated Regressors', *International Economic Review*, 25, 221–47.

A. Pagan, A. D. Hall and P. K. Trivedi (1983) 'Assessing the Variability of Inflation', *Review of Economic Studies*, 50, 585–96.

J. M. Parkin (1970) 'Discount House Portfolio and Debt Selection Behaviour', *Review of Economic Studies*, 37, 469–97.

J. M. Parkin, M. R. Gray and R. J. Barrett (1970) 'The Portfolio Behaviour of Commercial Banks', in K. Hilton and D. F. Heathfield (eds), *The Econometric Study of the UK*, London: Macmillan.

A. W. Phillips (1954) 'Stabilisation Policy in a Closed Economy', *Economic Journal*, 64, 290–323.

A. W. Phillips (1957) 'Stabilisation Policy and the Time Forms of Lagged Responses', *Economic Journal*, 67, 265–77.

W. F. Sharpe (1985) *Investments*, Englewood Cliffs, N.J.: Prentice-Hall International.

P. D. Spencer (1981) 'A Model of the Demand for British Government Stocks by Non-Bank Residents 1967–77', *Economic Journal*, 91, 938–60.

J. Tobin (n.d.) 'Properties of Assets' (chapter 2 of an unpublished manuscript).

H. Wills (1979) 'Inferring Expectations', London: LSE (unpublished).

Part II
Special Problems

5 Tax Effects in Gilt-edged Security Valuation

Robert G. Luther and J. Matatko

The central problem of bond (and general cash flow) management is the valuation of the sequence of temporal cash flows generated by the bond. One approach (see, e.g., Brennan and Schwartz, 1979) postulates a stochastic process for bond price dynamics and obtains an equilibrium pricing relationship. An earlier but still popular approach assumes certainty of expectations on the part of bond holders and assigns the value of the bond as the sum of the discounted cash flows. To perform this calculation it is necessary, however, to apply an appropriate discount function. The estimation of this discount function has in turn produced many studies (see, e.g., McCulloch, 1975; Jordan, 1984). This problem is compounded by the existence of different tax rates for income and capital gains and of varying marginal rates of income tax among individuals and corporations. This paper adopts the second approach and addresses the problem of term structure estimation in the presence of tax effects. It also reviews the development of the current system of taxation of investors in the UK government securities market with particular reference to the anomalous low-coupon issues.

Schaefer (1981; 1982), in widely referenced papers, applied a linear programming methodology to the market for British government bonds. The results[1] indicated the existence of tax clienteles for different bonds, the clientele being formed by investors lying within a particular tax bracket. Although the primal/dual formulation used by Schaefer is elegant, the approach has several difficulties. First, as pointed out by Jordan (1984), without the assumption of no random 'errors' in bond prices, the linear programming approach produces valuation bias. Secondly, as acknowledged by Schaefer, the solution of the linear programming problem for the discount function makes the discount factors a function of the problem's parameters. Since these parameters include the specified tax rate, the discount function will in general be forced to vary functionally with the tax rate.[2] There seems to be little reason, *a priori*, to suppose such dependence exists.

Lastly, examination of the examples shown by Schaefer (1981; 1982) reveals considerable instability in tax clienteles' tax brackets, even in adjacent months.

An alternative popular approach (see, e.g., McCulloch, 1975; Jordan, 1984; Fong and Vasicek, 1982) has been to specify a functional form for the discount function, apply unspecified tax rates to the various bond cash flows and jointly estimate an income tax rate and the parameters of the discount function. The usual (generalised) least-squares approach selects that set of tax rates and other parameter values which 'fit' the observed data more closely than any other single set of estimates. This approach selects a single discount function, which does not depend directly on tax rates. It also selects only a single set of tax rates. The specification of a single tax rate, however, denies the existence of tax clienteles. The estimated tax rates are, presumably, to be interpreted as some average unspecified form, of tax rates across different bond clienteles. Litzenberger and Rolfo (1984) in particular apply this approach to the UK bond market, in the context of a broader international study of tax effects on bond prices.

In this study we use the general approach of McCulloch, and Litzenberger and Rolfo, but this paper

1. allows both income tax and effective capital gains tax rates to be estimated, and
2. presents results for bonds subsidivided into possible 'clientele groupings'.

The approach is applied to data on British government securities at a single time point. The UK tax regime has shown substantial variation over time (see below; also see Poterba and Summers, 1984a; 1984b for a similar point made in relation to common stock returns) and correct evaluation of tax effects, at each point in time, is plainly necessary to predict the effect of such changes.

TAX REGIMES 1965–88

Much of the prominent literature (for example Schaefer, 1981; Schaefer, 1982; Litzenberger and Rolfo, 1984) in the field of UK security valuation has implied tax structures very much less complicated than they in reality are. Furthermore, the extent to which the

Table 5.1 Features of UK tax rates arising from investment in gilts, November 1988

Investor category	*% tax borne on* Capital gains (%)	Income (%)
Pension funds	0	0
Traders	35	35
Banks and building societies	35	35
Individuals (lower rate)	0	25
Individuals (higher rate)	0	40
Lloyds premium trust funds	0	53
Companies	0	35
Insurance companies (life business)	0	35
Insurance companies (other business)	35	35

tax status of investors, and the tax treatment of specific transactions, is contingent upon the vagaries of transient legislation and Inland Revenue interpretation has been understated.

A comprehensive survey of all the details of past tax regimes would not be useful to this paper, and we will limit ourselves to commenting on some of the more interesting and relevant issues over the period 1965–88. The main features of UK tax rates applying at the selected time point of November 1988 are shown in Table 5.1.

There were significant changes to the tax structure following the Labour Party's election victory in 1964. Of particular interest was the introduction of capital gains tax from April 1965. Realised capital gains above an annual exemption level were taxed at a maximum rate of 30 per cent for the twenty-three years from 1965 to April 1988. The effective charge on capital gains was variable but, on limited amounts, could be significantly less. This was due to the existence of the 'alternative charge' system whereby half of the gains in any year (up to £5,000) could be treated as unearned income assessable to income tax; this dispensation continued until 1978. Capital gains made by companies were taxed as chargeable gains at the same 30 per cent, but were included in corporation tax.

From 1965 until 1969 holders of UK government securities were liable for tax on both coupon receipts (through income tax or corporation tax) and on realised capital gains (through capital gains tax or corporation tax). The gains made by dealers in securities are not of a capital nature and so are taxed at the normal rates of income tax and corporation tax.

In general, taxes on gains have been less onerous than taxes on income due to:

- lower rates,
- annual exemptions,
- flexibility as to the timing of the crystallisation, and, indeed,
- the theoretical ability to postpone such crystallisation indefinitely.

From March 1969 capital gains and losses (as defined for tax purposes) derived from trading in government securities were exempted from tax provided the securities had been held for at least 12 months prior to disposal. It is important to note that where such gains accrued to dealers, banks, building societies, and part of the business of insurance companies they were treated as income and were subject to income tax and corporation tax at normal rates – i.e., not all capital gains to holders of gilts were tax-exempt.[3] Since July 1986 the 12-month restriction has been removed. It can be seen that the distinction between capital gains and income gains arising from gilts has for many years been significant; for any given level of pre-tax return, a gilt with a higher proportion of its return in the form of capital gain was more attractive than a gilt yielding higher-coupon income.

Furthermore, because of the tax differentials there has been at various times a strong incentive to change income into capital (e.g., by buying ex-div and selling cum-div). The most important changes affecting short-term traders were introduced in the 1970 Finance Act prior to which 'dividend stripping' by trading around ex-days was widespread. The 1970 legislation empowered the Inland Revenue to void, for tax purposes, such trading if it reduced an individual's tax liability in any year by 10 per cent or more. Where there is a segmented market, unless there are legal or transaction-cost barriers, potential profits are available from arbitrage between segments. The legislation thus sought to close the loophole whereby organisations that were totally tax-exempt were making arbitrage profits – trading around ex-days can now attract taxes on income in spite of an institution's tax-exempt status. Other potential arbitrageurs, the traders, are also subject to anti-avoidance legislation which removed the incentive for short-term trading. In general, quoting Porterba and Summers (1984): 'The interactions among these tax provisions are

Table 5.2 Estimated distribution of UK government stocks

	Up to 5 years to maturity (%)	*More than 5 years to maturity (%)*
Building societies	19.0	1.0
Overseas investors	18.5	10.0
Individuals	16.0	9.0
Insurance companies	9.5	37.0
Banks and monetary sector	5.5	6.5
Industrial/commercial companies	4.5	1.0
Pension funds	3.0	28.5
Investment and unit trusts	1.0	1.0
Other	23.0	6.0
Total	£37.7 m	£96.9 m

Source: *Bank of England Quarterly Bulletin* (November 1988).

difficult to describe, and the extent to which the Board of Inland Revenue exercises its authority remains unclear. However, one cannot doubt that the opportunities for avoiding taxes by trading around ex-days were substantially reduced in 1970.'

Against this background the widespread issue of low-coupon gilts, which started in 1973 and occurred regularly between 1979 and 1988, is an anomaly. These low-coupon gilts were issued paying nominal rates of 2.5 per cent and 3.0 per cent and have been of short duration, typically five years or less, compared with an average of some ten years for gilts issued at par. In the period 1980 to 1986, the annual government revenue raised by sales of low-coupon gilts averaged about £1 bn amounting to between 5 per cent and 10 per cent of the total revenue from gilt sales. These issues had, to a large extent, been redeemed by the date of our study (November 1988), but those remaining are conspicuous by the relatively low pre-tax yields they offer. We have been unable to obtain a sectoral analysis of the ownership of individual gilt issues, but some indication of how the low-coupon gilts are held is given by Table 5.2. An analysis of all market holdings of gilts shows the following results.

The difference in composition between the first column (which includes all of the low-coupon short-dated stocks) and the second in Table 5.2 is quite remarkable. Clearly, the tax consequences are only some of the factors influencing the investment policy of the various institutions.[4] A brief review of salient aspects of the taxation of the more significant participants shown above is given in Appendix 2.

In general one might expect *after-tax yields* for any maturity band to be approximately equal across differing levels of coupon; even if investors were not always maximising the after-tax yield one would expect primary dealers to keep the net yields in equilibrium. Discussions with practitioners indicate that this is generally so, but that since the proceeds of short sales are released only if the 'paper' is delivered, successful arbritrage requires the borrowing of paper from genuine investors. Because low-coupon stock is apparently largely held by individuals (often in relatively small blocks) and Lloyds premium trustees (who to date have been prohibited from lending securities) these specific issues are frequently 'inefficiently' priced.

Because of the tax differentials discussed earlier, these short-dated low-coupon gilts were attractive in general, but especially so to investors with higher marginal rates of income tax. The work of Hills (1984) and Saunders (1984) demonstrated that there was a tax clientele effect in the gilts market due to the existence of gilts with differing coupons and that the government sold low-coupon gilts specially designed for the high tax rate clientele. This is of course particularly ironic as these issues coincided with a period of top tax rates which varied between 60 per cent and 98 per cent over the period 1973 to 1986.

The reason for these issues was, naturally, that they allowed government to raise a larger capital sum for any given level of interest payments. The proportion of tax payers who paid tax at the top rate was not high but their total invested wealth was significant.[5] That the government was deliberately aiming to maintain and roll-over the debt held by this clientele is shown by their convenient packaging. First, it can be seen that the issue of low-coupon gilts was frequently made when another of these instruments was about to mature. Secondly, it can be seen that tax avoidance was facilitated by the existence of the 'three-week period'. During the three-week period prior to the ex-div date, contracts between sellers and buyers could be agreed either cum-div or ex-div. This allowed investors to hold a stock for fractionally longer than 12 months (thus avoiding capital gains tax in the 1984 to 1986 period), and yet capitalise one of every two six-monthly coupon distributions.

While these strategies were permitted, related tax avoidance was being practised in the form of bond-washing, and by the use of deep discount corporate bonds. The accrued income rule, which was adopted in 1985, removed the benefit from these activities. This rule correctly identifies the accrued income element of any bond purchased and this is then treated as income for tax purposes in the hands of the seller and likewise abates the buyers' first coupon received.[6] Interestingly, gilts series that were already in issue were not covered by this rule, nor are any further tranches of existing gilts (e.g., 6 per cent Funding Loan 1993 could still be issued). Given the current thinking evidenced by the early redemptions of the national debt this option is unlikely to be exercised.

A major change has come since April 1988 with the aggregation of capital gains made by private individuals with income for tax purposes. For basic rate taxpayers this has reduced the rate of tax on capital gains from 30 per cent to 25 per cent but, more significantly, most large capital gains are now taxed not at 30 per cent but at 40 per cent; the rate differential between tax on capital gains and income has been removed. This will not remove the attractiveness of low-coupon gilts since the capital gains on these instruments remain tax-exempt; nor will it affect the tax on chargeable gains, but it does remove the principal reason for individuals' preference for capital gains as opposed to income.[7] For a more detailed analysis of relevant aspects of current taxation and investment policies of various institutions and groups, refer to Appendix 2.

STATISTICAL METHODOLOGY AND DATA

The problem addressed in this section is the specification of an observable model relating government security prices to the term structure of interest rates and tax rates. The approach to term structure estimation taken here follows broadly those of McCulloch (1975), Jordan (1984), Fong and Vasicek (1982), and Litzenberger and Rolfo (1984) (only the last-mentioned attempts to model UK data). The present study diverges from these (in particular, Litzenberger and Rolfo) by obtaining *estimates* of tax rates applicable to *both* capital gains and coupon payments. It also explicitly allows for the existence of tax clienteles in the UK government bond market (as demonstrated, e.g., by Schaefer, 1981; 1982).

The derivation of the basic equation used to model bond prices runs as follows (for a detailed discussion see, e.g., Schaefer, 1981 or most of the above references). Assuming a world of perfect certainty and capital market equilibrium the price of a bond, with no default risk, will simply be equal to the present value of the cash flows provided by the bond to its holders.

$$P_i = \sum_{j=0}^{M_i-1} \frac{C_i\,(1-\tau_I^i)}{(1+r(t_i+\frac{j}{2}))^{t_i+j/2}} + \frac{100-(100-P_i)\tau_G^i}{(1+r(t_i+\frac{M_i-1}{2}))^{t_i+\frac{M_i-1}{2}}} \tag{5.1}$$

where P_i is the price of bond i

C_i is the coupon payment of bond i

t_i is the time (in years) to the first coupon payment

M_i is the total number of coupon payments to be made

τ_I^i, τ_G^i are the marginal income and gains tax rates for the holders of bond i (assumed inter-temporally constant)

$r(t)$ is the spot interest rate applicable to money borrowed or lent for a period of t years.

(All the bonds considered in this study make payments at 6-monthly intervals. Therefore it is necessary in (5.1) only to specify the time in years elapsing before the first coupon payment and the number of payment to be made.)

Equation (5.1) is seen to be highly non-linear in the spot rates and to contain expected future tax rates. For simplicity we assume the tax rates applied by market participants are time-independent. We also reformulate equation (5.1) in terms of the discount function, $D(t)$, where

$$D(t) = \frac{1}{(1+r(t))^t} \tag{5.2}$$

making these substitutions gives

$$P_i = C(1-\tau_I^i)\sum_j D(t_i+\frac{j}{2}) + 100 - (100-P_i)\tau_G^i \times D\,(t_i+\frac{M_i-1}{2}) \tag{5.3}$$

Equation 5.3 is now linear in the discount function $D(t)$.

As equation (5.3) shows, the parameters to be estimated of $D(t)$, τ_I^i and τ_G^i are not identified (see Litzenberger and Rolfo, 1984 for a full discussion of this point). However, it is not desirable, even it were possible, to estimate the discount factors without restriction. Such estimates would be made at discrete points in time, since there exists only a finite number of bonds. The resulting sequence of estimates would, in general, be discontinuous. Discount factors required for arbitrary time points would not therefore be available. To circumvent this problem (and also that of identification of τ_I^i and τ_G^i) we approximate $D(t)$ by a smooth function of t. No strong *a priori* grounds are available to restrict the choice of function. McCulloch, Jordan, Litzenberger and Rolfo use cubic splines (see these references for discussions of the properties of these polynomials) while Fong and Vasicek recommend the use of exponential splines. Since we wish to compare our results with other findings for the UK gilts market we use cubic splines to approximate $D(t)$. Explicitly we take:

$$D(t) = 1 + \alpha t + \beta t^2 + \gamma_0 t^3 + \gamma_1 DV_1(t)(t - t_1^*)^3 + \gamma_2 DV_2(t)(t - t_2^*)^3 \quad (5.4)$$

where $DV_1(t)$ and $DV_2(t)$ are dummy variables shifting the cubic term of the polynomial for time points t_1^* and t_2^* respectively. Formally

$$DV_k(t) = 0 \quad t < t_k^* \quad k = 1, 2$$
$$= 1 \quad \text{otherwise}$$

(The points t_k^* are known as knot points for the cubic spline. 'Smoothness' constraints require the lower-order coefficients not to shift.) The choice of values for the knot points is arbitrary, as indeed is their number. We simply select two values $t_1^* = 5$ years, $t_2^* = 15$ years, since these points are usually cited by market participants as marking the divisions between 'shorts', 'mediums' and 'longs'.

When equation (5.4) is substituted into (5.3), the equation for P is:

$$P = W(M + \alpha\sum h_j + \beta\sum h_j^2 + \gamma_0\sum h_j^3 + \gamma_1\sum DV_1(h_j)(h_j - t_1^*)^3 + \gamma_2\sum DV_2(h_j)(h_j - t_1^*)^3)$$
$$+ Z(1 + \alpha h_{M-1} + \beta h_{M-1}^2 + \gamma_0 h_{M-1}^3 + \gamma_1 DV_1(h_{M-1})(h_{M-1} - t_1^*)^3 + \gamma_2 DV_2(h_{M-1})(h_{M-1} - t_2^*)^3)$$
$$+ U \quad (5.5)$$

where $W = C(1 - \tau_I)$, $Z = 100 - \tau_G(100 - P)$, $h_j = t + j/2$ and the subscript i has been omitted for convenience.

Equation (5.5) produces the starting point for the estimation reported below. Equation (5.5) is non-linear, because of taxation, in its coefficients but even so it is estimated as formulated in (5.5). The variable Z contains the endogenous variable P and hence contains a stochastic error component correlated with u producing an errors-in-variable problem (also, as it stands, plainly the best fitting equation for (5.5) would simply set $\tau_G = 1$ and all other coefficients $= 0$).

To allow effective estimation, three approaches are followed here:

Pre-specifying τ_I and τ_G

If τ_I and τ_G are pre-specified at appropriate levels, the equation becomes linear in the remaining coefficients. If τ_G is set to equal zero, on the erroneous grounds that the effective tax rate is, in this situation equal to zero, the errors-in-variables problem disappears. (Litzenberger and Rolfo effectively approach the problem by eliminating τ_G from the RHS of equation (5.5). This has the unfortunate effect of preventing the estimation of τ_G.)

Using an Instrumental Variable for P

In this approach P is replaced by an instrument, $\hat{P}$ say, where P is uncorrelated with the disturbance term in equation (5.5). Using an analogy with two-stage least squares in a single equation setting, $\hat{P}$ was formed from a regression of P on the exogenous variables C and h_{m-1}, the coupon and maturity of each bond.

Solving for P – Maximum Likelihood Estimation

Since equation (5.5) can be viewed as a single equation involving a single unknown, P, it can be solved for that unknown. The resulting formulation for P is

$$P = \frac{1}{(1 - \tau_G f(.))}[Wg(.) + 100\,(1 - \tau_G)f(.)] + e \qquad (5.6)$$

where $f(.)$ and $g(.)$ are respectively the polynomial coefficient s of Z and W in equation (5.5).

Equation (5.6) is highly non-linear in the tax rates τ_g and τ_I. It does, however, provide estimates jointly of both these rates and of the coefficients of the discount function, without the rather artificial device of an instrumental variable, as used above.

The Properties of the Disturbance Term

In order to estimate and draw inferences about the coefficients of the discount function in any of the three approaches described above, some assumptions are required about the distribution of the disturbance team. First, it might generally be expected to be heteroscedastic with P. Secondly, this situation is complicated if the disturbance is introduced through the cubic approximation to $D(t)$; the disturbance becomes a function of all the variables on the RHS of equation (5.5). Lastly, the solution of equation (5.5) to obtain (5.6) further complicates the properties of the disturbance on the RHS variables. In view of the rather involved and intractable nature of this dependency, together with the fact that the disturbance also results generally from the fact that we are *estimating* tax rates and coefficients, we initially take the simplest route of relying on the central limit theorems and assume the disturbances are normal i.i.d.. Given the normality assumption we are able to proceed to tests of significance on coefficients and maximum likelihood estimation of the non-linear forms such as equations (5.5) and (5.6). Maximum likelihood also results in estimates of the standard errors of the coefficients. (This is particularly important since the iterative method of Litzenberger and Rolfo and McCulloch does not produce these indicators of the accuracy of estimates).

Data

The data consists of the prices of all non-index-linked, finite maturity government bonds outstanding on 30 November 1988. The estimates reported in this paper are illustrative and are presented simply for one single day. One simplification was introduced into the estimation process. For those stocks with variable maturity dates, the maturity date was chosen to be the earliest maturity date for those selling above par, the latest for those selling below par. This simplification appears to be almost universally adopted by practitioners.

EMPIRICAL RESULTS

In this section we present three sets of results based on the specifications set out in the previous section.

Imposed Tax Regimes

Table 5.3 shows the estimates of the coefficients α, β, γ, γ_1, γ_2, of the discount function (5.4) corresponding to three significant tax categories (i.e., pension funds, higher rate individuals and dealers paying corporation tax on income and capital gains). Regressions are performed four times for each regime:

1. With and without the coefficient of $MC(1 - \tau_I)$ in equation (5.5) restricted to be +1 (This is implicit in the formulation (5.5)).
2. With and without low-coupon bonds. These are widely cited as evidence of clientele effects (e.g., Schaefer, 1982; Saunders, 1984).

Reviewing Table 5.3, the main features are:

1. The coupon coefficient varies significantly in all cases from unity, the value pre-specified.
2. The coefficients of the discount polynomial vary in both size and sign depending on the tax regime chosen.
3. The coefficient γ_2, the shift in the cubic term for the longest bonds, is uniformly positive and significant, indicating a market relative preference for these bonds.

Instrumental Variable (IV) and Maximum Likelihood (ML) Estimates

The IV and ML estimates shown in Tables 5.4 and 5.5 are based on equations (5.5) and (5.6) above, and permit estimates of both income and capital gains tax rates implied by the data. To examine for possible tax clientele effects, results are also provided with bonds subdivided by coupon yield. Only one set of ML estimates is presented. For all other cases (an attempt was made to replicate the estimates of Table 5.4) it was found that the surface of the likelihood function was very 'flat' and spurious maxima were found, corresponding to highly implausible parameter values.

Table 5.3 Linear regressions

Tax regime	*Included bonds*	*Coupon* coefficient	$\hat{\alpha}$	$\hat{\beta}$	$\hat{\gamma}$	$\hat{\gamma}_1$	$\hat{\gamma}_2$	R^2	N
A $T_I = 0$ $T_G = 0$	All	–	–0.64*(–1)	0.19(–3)	0.27(–3)	–0.44(–3)	0.26*(–3)	0.997	87
$T_I = 0$ $T_G = 0$	All	1.21*	–0.11*	0.89*(–2)	–0.29(–3)	0.13(–3)	0.24*(–3)	0.947	87
$T_I = 0$ $T_G = 0$	Coupon > 5%	–	–0.63*(–1)	–0.20*(–3)	0.30(–3)	–0.47(–3)	0.26(–3)	0.997	80
$T_I = 0$ $T_G = 0$	Coupon > 5%	1.27*	–0.12	0.11*(–1)	–0.43(–3)	0.27(–3)	0.20*(–3)	0.947	80

Note: * In both cases, Chow tests significant at 5 per cent level.

B $T_I = 0.4$ $T_G = 0$	All	–	–0.24*(–1)	0.16*(–1)	0.14*(–2)	–0.15*(–2)	0.32*(–3)	0.98	87
$T_I = 0.4$ $T_G = 0$	All	2.02*	–0.12*	0.89*(–2)	–0.30*(–3)	0.13(–3)	0.24*(–3)	0.95	87
$T_I = 0.4$ $T_G = 0$	Coupon > 5%	–	–0.25*(–1)	–0.17*(–3)	0.14*(–3)	–0.16*(–2)	0.34*(–3)	0.98	80
$T_I = 0.4$ $T_G = 0$	Coupon > 5%	2.11*	–0.12	0.11*(–1)	–0.43*(–3)	0.27(–3)	0.21*(–3)	0.96	80
C $T_I = 0.35$ $T_G = 0.35$	All	–	–0.19(–1)	0.17*(–1)	0.14*(–2)	–0.16*(–2)	0.32*(–3)	0.98	87
$T_I = 0.35$ $T_G = 0.35$	All	1.8*	–0.11*(–1)	0.37(–2)	0.86(–4)	0.26(–3)	0.22*(–3)	0.95	87
$T_I = 0.35$ $T_G = 0.35$	Coupon > 5%	–	–0.20(–1)	–0.17*(–1)	0.15*(–2)	–0.16(–2)	0.33*(–3)	0.98	80
$T_I = 0.35$ $T_G = 0.35$	Coupon > 5%	1.90*	–0.12*	0.61(–2)	–0.92(–4)	–0.61(4)	0.17*(–3)	0.95	80

Notes: Figures in parentheses beside entries show the power of 10 by which each figure is to be multiplied.
* Indicates coefficient significant at the 5 per cent level.

Reviewing the estimates in Tables 5.4 and 5.5, we found two important facts.

Implied Income and Capital Gains Tax Rates

When all bonds are pooled together the ML estimates show what appear to be plausible 'average' values for T_I and T_G, with $T_I \simeq 25$ per cent and the average capital gains tax rate, $T_G \simeq 5$ per cent. The standard errors of both parameter estimates are relatively large. In general the IV estimates, which are shown with bonds subdivided by coupon yield, are less satisfactory with obvious instability in estimates due to the large number of parameters being estimated, relative to the available number of data points (line 4 of Table 5.4 is based on only 11 observations, 7 bonds with coupons less than 5 per cent). The capital gains tax rates, although with large standard errors, show an acceptable pattern: the higher rate is always on the higher coupon bond set. This does not consistently apply to the income tax rate estimates: the estimated rate for coupons above 10 per cent is higher than for those below 10 per cent. This effect may simply be a product of the variability of the parameter estimates for the reason discussed above.

Term Structure Estimates

Although, as Table 5.4 shows, estimated tax rates differ widely between different sets of bonds, the estimates of the coefficients of the discount function appear stable. Ignoring line 4 (based on 11 observations) the estimates of α, β and γ are all seen to be significant, of the same sign and of the same order of magnitude. The ML estimates on Table 5.5 agree in these terms with the IV estimates of Table 5.4 The general lack of significance in the γ_1 and γ_2 estimates seems to indicate that the 'long-bond' effect, noted above, disappears when tax rates are explicitly introduced into the estimation procedure.

SUMMARY AND CONCLUSIONS

This paper has considered the problem of estimating the term structure of interest rates, under certainty, when tax clientele effects are taken into account. The UK tax system is seen to allow several different rates for income and effective capital gains tax on govern-

Table 5.4 Instrumental variable estimates

Bonds included	T_I	T_G	$\hat{\alpha}$	$\hat{\beta}$	$\hat{\gamma}$	$\hat{\gamma}_1$	$\hat{\gamma}_2$	N
All	0.18*	–0.69(–1)	–0.84(–1)	0.35*(–2)	–0.57*(–4)	–0.14(–3)	0.14(–3)	87
	(0.03)	0.35(–1)						
Coupon > 5.0%	.25*	.15*	–0.76*(–1)	0.30*(–2)	–0.49*(–4)	0.53	0.32	80
	(.04)	(.07)						
Coupon > 7.0%	.24*	.19	–0.90(–1)	.47*(–2)	–10*(–3)	.12*(–4)	.76*(–3)	76
	(.06)	(.12)						
Coupon < 7.0%	.64*	.06*	–.62(–1)	–.29*(–2)	.13*(–2)	–.80*(–2)	.89*	11
	(.06)	(.01)						
Coupon > 9.0%	.25*	.11	–.90*(–1)	.53*(–2)	–.17*(–3)	.46(–3)	–.23(–2)	40
	(.09)	(.17)						
Coupon < 9.0%	.37*	.05	–.82*(–1)	.41*(–2)	–.93*(–4)	.93(–4)	.10(–3)	20
	(.05)	(.04)						
Coupon > 10.0%	.43*	.37	–.89*(–1)	.94*(–2)	–.51*(–3)	.25(–2)	–.11(–1)	45
	(.11)	(.21)						
Coupon < 10.0%	0.31*	.05	–.84*(–1)	.43*(–1)	–.97*(–4)	.44(–4)	.43*(–3)	42
	(0.04)	(.03)						

Notes: Figures in parentheses below the estimates for T_I and T_G are standard errors.
* indicates a coefficient significant at the 5 per cent level.

Table 5.5 Maximum likelihood (ML) estimates

Bonds included	T_I	T_G	$\hat{\alpha}$	$\hat{\beta}$	$\hat{\gamma}$	$\hat{\gamma}_1$	$\hat{\gamma}_2$
All	0.24*	0.05	–0.77*(–1)	0.31*(–2)	–0.52*(–4)	0.89(–6)	0.82(–4)

Note: * indicates a coefficient significant at the 5 per cent level.

ment securities. The fact that capital gains tax is zero for such bonds does not mean that all such gains are untaxed. Empirical estimates of implied rates for *both* taxes were found using different estimation techniques and specifications. These estimates were made jointly with estimates of a polynomial approximation to the term structure.

We are able to draw the following conclusions:

- The derivation of the term structure is improved by jointly estimating the term structure and investors' tax rates applicable to income and capital gains. We have presented a model to allow this joint estimation.
- There is some evidence of an unarbitraged disequilibrium indicated by the market preference for bonds of more than 15 years to maturity. This supports the view that the maturity preferences may be of primary influence and yields of only secondary importance, and that there are constraints upon arbitrage activity. The 'long bonds' are largely held by pension funds and insurance companies while the 'short market' is dominated by building societies, individuals and overseas investors.
- The estimates of effective rates of tax (see Table 5.5) across all gilt issues are 5 per cent and 25 per cent for capital gains and income respectively. Being averages, these values are meaningful only in showing that tax on gains (borne by traders, banks, etc.) do have some limited influence on prices, and secondly, that the range of tax rates on income (from 0 per cent for pension funds to 53 per cent for other participants) is reflected in an average tax penalty on income of some 25 per cent. The practice of assuming away all tax on capital gains is shown to be misleading.
- We give further evidence of the tax clientele effect in UK gilts. The results are consistent with higher-coupon issues being held by lower tax rate investors, and vice versa.
- Finally, our review of the tax regime has shown that government encouraged and exploited tax avoidance by the wealthy. It is not clear that this resulted in a lower total cost of borrowing than had the funds been raised by issues at par. While the accrued income rule has precluded tax avoidance by trading around coupon dates, the capital gain by low-coupon issues to redemption remains a vestigial anomaly.

Appendix 1 Early Simple Models Which Worked Towards a Method of Inferring the Tax Rates of Investors in Specific Securities

Both approaches are of limited usefulness in that they allow estimation of only one of the two tax rates after having assumed a value for the other. Most of the studies which made use of these models have worked under the restrictive assumption that effective rates of tax on capital gains approximates zero. Thus no account is taken of the very real tax consequences of realised capital gains, nor of the tax treatment of dealers, who clearly have a significant influence on security pricing.

It is also noted, with reference to this paper, that neither of the approaches described below has any necessary relation to the issue of term structure estimation.

1. Following the Elton and Gruber (1970) approach one may infer the income tax rate of a clientele holding an equity and *assuming tax on capital gains at 30 per cent.*

Example

$$P(\text{cum}) - (P(\text{cum}) - PO)^{*}Tcg = P(\text{ex}) + D^{*}(1 - Ti) - (P(\text{ex}) - PO)^{*}Tcg$$

where P = price, cum or ex, and PO is the price at which equity was purchased
Tcg = rate of tax on capital gains
Ti = rate of tax on income
D = dividend

If, say, PO = 50
$P(\text{cum})$ = 100
$P(\text{ex})$ = 90
D = 15
Tcg = 30%

Then by substitution into the equation it can be inferred that *Ti* = 53 per cent.

2. Similarly, in the US 'It has been common to measure the spread between yields on taxable and tax-exempt bonds of maturity *Ti* in terms of the implicit tax rate:

$$Q(iT) = 1 - Y(mT)/Y(eT)$$

where *Y(mt)* and *Y(et)* denote the yield to maturity on tax-exempt and taxable bonds of maturity *T'* (Kochin and Parks (1988).

By rearranging the equation we get:

$$(1 - Q(iT)) = Y(mT)/Y(eT)$$

to reform a hypothesis that since the tax on income of 'natural holders' of, say, short-dated low-coupon gilts is 40 per cent we would expect the ratio of yields (i.e., *Y(mT)/Y(eT)*) to be 60 per cent.

3. A small point to note is that stocks will be priced on the basis of tax expectations, and that therefore the implied tax rate is the expected marginal tax rate of the marginal investor. Following this line of argument, we might test whether implied tax rates could be used as a lead indicator of changes in tax legislation or rates.

Appendix 2 Relevant Aspects of Taxation and Investment Policies of UK Institutions and Special Interest Groups

PENSION FUNDS

Approved pension funds are not liable to income tax or capital gains tax. The critical issue is therefore the gross yield. Practitioners have observed what appears to be an increase in 'tactical' investment by pension funds (i.e., increasingly active investment management and less concentration upon the simple matching of investment maturity dates which liabilities (which are mainly long-term)).

BUILDING SOCIETIES AND BANKS

Building societies now, like banks, pay corporation tax at the same rates as general commercial companies (i.e., currently at 35 per cent). Until February 1984 building societies had a special corporation tax rate of 40 per cent, and had their gains made on gilts treated as capital gains.

After obtaining legal advice, the Inland Revenue decided to treat gains of building societies arising from the sale of gilts after February 1984 as part of trading profits and not as chargeable gains, putting them on an equal footing with banks. This would appear to remove any incentive for building societies to make use of the element of capital gain in short-dated low-coupon gilts; in fact, since these yield *lower* pre-tax rates, one might assume that building societies would not trade in these instruments.

From the table of sectoral holdings (Table 5.2) it can be seen that banks and building societies invest heavily in issues with less than five years to maturity, presumably the higher-yielding ones. Like most investors in the gilts market the principal concern is risk avoidance; banks and building societies are 'cash denominated' organisations and their investment pattern reflects this. Under the Building Societies Act 1986, building societies are able to convert to companies, but as yet only the Abbey National has followed this course.

INVESTMENT TRUSTS

Since 1980 the capital gains made by investment trusts (ITs) in dealing in investments are not treated as chargeable gains, but the gains made by the investors in the trusts are. ITs have always obtained relief for the income tax withheld from franked income they receive, provided they pass on that income to their own shareholders.

UNIT TRUSTS

The capital gains made by unit trusts in dealing in investments are not treated as chargeable gains, but the gains made by the investors in the trusts are.

LLOYDS PREMIUM TRUST FUNDS

These trust funds amount to some £2,000m to £3,000m and the investments need to be relatively liquid and low risk. The total market value of gilts with up to five years to maturity in March 1988 was £41,000 million. Income from these funds is subject to income tax, based upon the taxable incomes of the names comprising the syndicates. The accounts of these syndicates are prepared on a rolling three-year basis and the effective tax rate on income in any year may be approximated as the average of the tax rates of the current and previous two years. Thus income earned late in 1988 would be subject to tax at a rate of

$$(40\% + 60\% + 60\%) / 3 = 53\%.$$

By investing in short-dated low-coupon gilts the syndicates can get the bulk of their yield in the form of tax-exempt capital gains. Frequency and volume of dealing in instruments does not necessarily imply that one is dealing for profit; this is especially so if the investments are held to maturity, so these funds can use these vehicles profitably.

LIFE INSURANCE OFFICES

These are taxed in the same way as normal commercial-industrial companies. The major aim of their investment policy is to match the maturity of investments with the crystallising of their liabilities. In much of 1988 and 1989 the slope of the yield curve was negative and higher yields were available from short-dated issues, but the incentive to obtain these yields is strongly opposed by concern to avoid risk arising from 'term mismatch' (e.g., if an insurance company did aim to cover long-term liabilities with short-term investments and interest rates did fall, the cost of subsequently buying into long-term investments would rise, and significantly so for a long-term issue where a high proportion of the value was the capitalised coupons).

The investment activities of general insurance business is taxed in the same way as banks, building societies and traders.

OVERSEAS INVESTORS

One would assume that investors based in other countries would be motivated to buy gilts that are interest-exempt from British tax to non-residents. This category comprises:

- 13% Treasury Stock 1990
- 8.25% Treasury Loan 1990
- 12.75% Treasury Loan 1992
- 12.5% Treasury Loan 1993
- 6% Funding Loan 1993
- 13.75% Treasury Loan 1993
- 14.5% Treasury Loan 1993
- 9% Treasury Loan 1994
- 12.75% Treasury Loan 1995
- 9% Treasury Loan 1992–6
- 3.5%
- 15.25% Treasury Loan 1996
- 13.25% Exchequer Loan 1996
- 13.25% Treasury Loan 1997
- 8.75% Treasury Loan 1997
- 6.75% Treasury Loan 1995–8
- 15.5% Treasury Loan 1995
- 9.5% Treasury Loan 1999
- 8% Treasury Loan 2002–6
- 5.5% Treasury Stock 2008–12
- 7.75% Treasury Loan 2012–15

War Loan (this loan is also attractive to certain domestic investors in that interest is paid gross (i.e., before deduction of tax).

The holdings of overseas investors are largely in short-dated stocks as flexibility, coupled with avoidance of variability arising out of interest rate fluctuation, is relatively more important because the investment is often mainly a vehicle for taking a view on currency exchange rates.

HIGH INCOME INDIVIDUALS

The income earned by individuals in the latter part of 1988 was subject to income tax at 40 per cent to the extent that it exceeded £19,300 per annum. Reference to *Inland Revenue Statistics* (1986) shows that some £21,000 m of government securities are held by individuals, and that this account for 3 per cent of the total net capital value of identified wealth (excludes rights accruing from pension schemes and assets excluded from probate, such as discretionary trusts). Of the wealthiest 3 in every 1,000 of adult population (identified personal wealth exceeding £100,00) 56 per cent included gilts in their portfolio, with an aggregate value for this group of £10,000 m.

Since the majority of these wealthy individuals are subject to tax on income at 40 per cent, it might be expected that the bulk of the £10,000 m would be attracted towards short-dated low-coupon gilts in view of their fiscal privilege. The total market value of gilts in November 1988 was £135,000 m, of which £38,000 m comprised issues with up to five years to maturity (*Bank of England Quarterly Bulletin*, November 1988).

Notes

1. Of course, in order for such a clientele model to yield an equilibrium it is necessary to assume the existence of market frictions, in particular a no short-sales constraint.
2. The authors are grateful to David Oakes for this point.
3. If they were, the income tax rates of investors could easily be inferred by use of the models described in Appendix 1.
4. Others include the fact that the market in the longer-dated gilts is relatively thin; that investors may wish to align the realisation of their investments with their exposure to making payments; and that, anyway, should one have to sell investments before the redemption date there is always a risk that one may suffer an unexpected loss.
5. Refer to Appendix 2, p. 000.
6. The accrued income rule applies only if the nominal value of a portfolio exceeds £5,000 for all of the year in question.
7. It has correctly been suggested in the financial press that this may be one of the factors that has caused dividend cover to be reduced since April 1988.

References

Bank of England (1988) *Bank of England Quarterly Bulletin* (November).

Brennan, M. and E. Schwartz (1979) 'A Continuous Time Approach to the Pricing of Bonds', *Journal of Banking & Finance* (July).

Dermody, J. C. and E. Z. Prisman (1988) 'Term Structure Multiplicity and Clientele in Markets with Transactions Costs and Taxes', *Journal of Finance* (September).

Elton, E. J. and M. J. Gruber (1970) 'Marginal Stockholders' Tax Rates and the Clientele Effect', *Review of Economics and Statistics* (February).

Fong, G. and O. Vasicek (1982) 'Term Structure Modelling', *Journal of Finance* (May).

Hills, J. (1984) *Taxation and Fiscal Privilege*, IFS Report Series, 9, London: Institute for Fiscal Studies.

Jordan, J. V. (1984) 'Tax Effects in Term Structure Estimation', *Journal of Finance*, 39 (June).

Kochin, L. A. and R. W. Parks (1988) 'Was the Tax-Exempt Market Inefficient or Were Future Expected Tax Rates Negative?', *Journal of Finance*, 43 (September).

Litzenberger, R. H. and J. Rolfo (1984) 'An International Study of Tax Effects on Government Bonds', *Journal of Finance*, 39 (March).

McCulloch, J. H. (1975) 'Tax Adjusted Yield Curves', *Journal of Finance* (June).

Poterba, J. and L. Summers (1984a) 'New Evidence That Taxes Affect the Valuation of Dividends', *Journal of Finance* 39 (December).

Poterba, J. and L. Summers (1984b) 'The Economic Effects of Dividend

Taxation', in *Recent Advances in Corporate Finance*, New York: Dow-Jones Irwin (1984).
Saunders, M. (1984) 'Tax Privileged Government Debt: Low Coupon Gilts', *Fiscal Studies* (May).
Schaefer, S. M. (1981) 'Measuring a Tax-Specific Term Structure of Interest Rates in the Market for British Government Securities', *Economic Journal*, 91 (June).
Schaefer, S. M. (1982) 'Tax-Induced Clientele Effects in the Market for British Government Securities', *Journal of Financial Economics* (July).

6 Why is There a Need for Interest Rate Management?

Charles Owen-Conway

The question that I wish to address in this paper is 'Why is there a need for Interest Rate Management?'

The graph in Figure 6.1 shows the extent of National Westminster Bank base rate movements over the period 1979–89. As you can see, interest rates are extremely volatile and a Finance Director/Treasurer has a major problem in drawing up budgets/cash flow forecasts in so far as deciding what rate to use in calculating the finance charge. This would have been particularly difficult in autumn 1988 when base rate moved from 7½ per cent to 13 per cent within a short period.

People generally have short memories and whilst interest rates were in single figures as recently as 3 July 1988, the average base rate for the 1984–9 years was in fact 11.04 per cent as at the end of August 1989. For 1979–89 this figures rises to 11.79 per cent. There is, therefore, a need for the Finance Director to take positive action to control such hard-hitting costs and any product/service that he can use to fix/limit interest costs must be examined.

In essence, along with sales the one line on a cash flow forecast over which a Finance Director may feel he has very little control, is the finance charge. He will know approximately what general overheads such as heating and lighting are going to be over the next year; labour rates are likely to have been agreed for a twelve-month period; is there a rent review due, etc.? The real concern, however, particularly now when rates are so high, is the effect of interest rates on profit performance. In our view and experience the Finance Director is looking to control interest rate exposure levels, provided this can be done simply and cheaply. He has in practice three choices (see Figure 6.2). We can regard these alternatives as a range across a spectrum: at one end there is inaction, although even inaction falls into two categories.

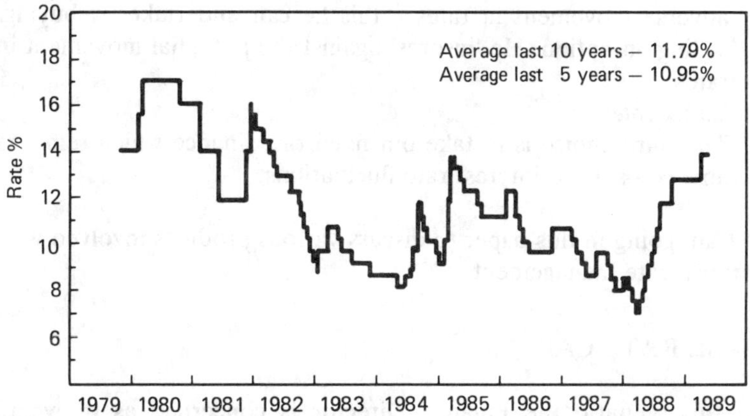

Source: NatWest Financial Services Section
Figure 6.1 NatWest base rate movements, 1 July 1979–30 June 1989

- Do nothing; live with the risk
- Buy options; insurance against adverse movements
- hedge completely; fix rates forward

Source: NatWest Financial Services Section
Figure 6.2 Strategic hedging alternatives

1. *To do nothing*

   To do nothing would be perfectly understandable for the Finance Director of a property company that anticipated selling properties in five months' time, and did not think that interest rates were going to increase but could he live with a rise of 2/3 per cent in interest rates should his perception be wrong? The greater problem, however, and regrettably one which surfaces all too often, is of the Finance Director who is too busy, does not understand the various interest rate management products available to him and does not want to know. He knows his own business but does not understand 'fancy' products and effectively buries his head in the sand.

2. *To enter interest rate options*

   The Finance Director who wishes to remain with floating interest rates, however, may want to limit the potential downside of any adverse movement in rates – this he can undertake by buying/selling an option. He 'insures' against the potential movement in rates.

3. *To fix rates*
   The third choice is to take out fixed rate finance which removes any exposure to interest rate fluctuations.

I am going in this paper to discuss various products involved with interest rate management.

BASE RATE CAP

In this scenario the Finance Director is concerned as to where interest rates are heading and wants to put some sort of limitation on the amount of interest that his company will pay. One alternative is for him to purchase a base rate cap.

Example 1 – interest rates increasing

- Base rate as at 15 September – 11 per cent.
- Customer does not wish to pay more than 12 per cent, excluding margin.
- Purchases a £1m cap (4 × £250,000) to take effect from 1 October at 11 per cent (strike rate).
- Pays first quarterly premium up-front.
- On 1 October base rate rises to 12 per cent – remains at 12 per cent until 31 December.
- At the end of December customer is paid 1 per cent on £1m for 3 months.

Note: Actual total borrowing costs will include premium payable plus margin.

Example 2 – interest rates falling

- Base Rate Cap at 11 per cent.
- Base Rate falls to 10 per cent 1 January and remains at 10 per cent until 31 March.
- Customer continues to pay the quarterly cap premium *but* pays only current rates, i.e., 10 per cent plus margin on the underlying borrowing.

– Enables customer to benefit from a 'downturn' in interest rates.

Note: Actual total borrowing costs will include premium payable plus margin.

Features

– Minimum amount: £250,000.
  Maximum £2,000,000.
– Term: Minimum 1 month.
  Maximum 2 years.
– Quarterly premiums in advance.
– Quarterly reimbursement in arrears.
– Not directly linked to borrowing.
– Deferred start caps available.

The ideal time to buy base rate caps is when rates are falling. The level of premium will be corresponding lower and the facility can be seen as the payment of 'insurance premium' for an 'insurance policy'. If, however, a corporation has no need of a 'cap' when rates are on the way down, then a 'cap', must be considered when rates are on the increase, although in so doing it must be appreciated that the premium will be correspondingly higher. National Westminster Bank is one of only a few banks offering interest rate caps linked to base rate.

LIBOR CAPS/COLLARS

A LIBOR (the London Inter-Bank Offered Rate) cap works in a very similar way to the base rate cap but certain features are slightly different.

– Amount: minimum £1m, maximum £100m.
– Term: up to 5 years.
– Premium payable in one amount up-front.
– Reimbursement in line with LIBOR fixture period.

By also putting a floor in place, the customer is effectively giving up the right to rates below a certain level and this has a value to the bank for, in the event that LIBOR rates fall below that floor rate, the customer will reimburse the bank with the difference on the nominal contract amount. The value of the floor reduces the cost of the premium for the cap and a cap and a floor taken together make a collar. If the value of the floor negates the premium due for the cap completely, this is called a nil cost collar.

INTEREST RATE CAPS

Benefits

- Protection against rising rates.
- Take advantage of falling rates.
- With a collar fees can be reduced (LIBOR only).
- Exercise an interest rate perception.

FORWARD BASE RATE AGREEMENTS (FBRAs)

One alternative to buying a base rate cap, an option, is to fix future interest rates by way of a forward base rate agreement.

Example

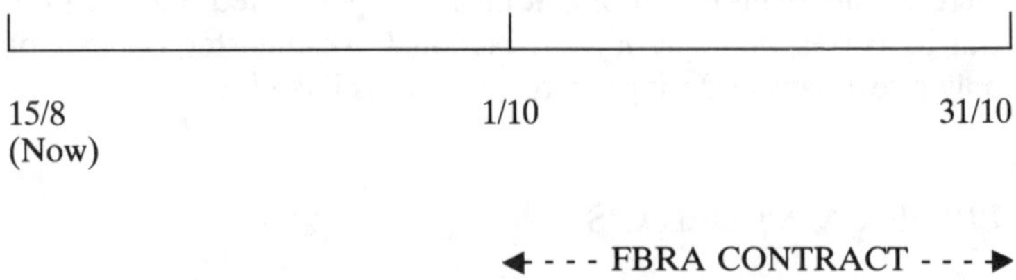

- Borrowing requirement £250,000 in October.
- Base rate now 10 per cent.
- Perception is that base rate will rise.
- Purchase FBRA contract, for which Bank quotes 10.5 per cent.

Settlement

- Base rate as at 1 October is 11 per cent and remains at 11 per cent until 31 October.
- Bank pays customer ½ per cent on £250,000 for 31 days. = £250,000 x 31/365 x ½ per cent = £106.16.
- If base rate had been 10 per cent throughout October, customer would pay Bank £106.16.

- Settlement made within 5 working days of 31 October.

Note: Customer continues to pay interest at base rate, i.e, 11 per cent, plus margin, throughout October on the underlying borrowing, but with the settlement under the FBRA the net rate is 10 per cent (plus margin).

Features

- Amount: minimum £250,000, maximum £20m. in units of £250,000.
- Term: each contract available for one calendar month; latest start date 12 months ahead; customer can have different contracts for different amounts.

Benefits

- Future borrowing costs can be fixed.
- Flexible cover for borrowing requirements.
- No up-front fee payable.
- Not linked to underlying borrowing.

LIBOR FORWARD RATE AGREEMENTS (FRA's)

LIBOR Forward Rate Agreements are similar to FBRAs but are quoted in line with the fixture period taken out on the underlying borrowing, with a minimum contract amount of £lm.

Example

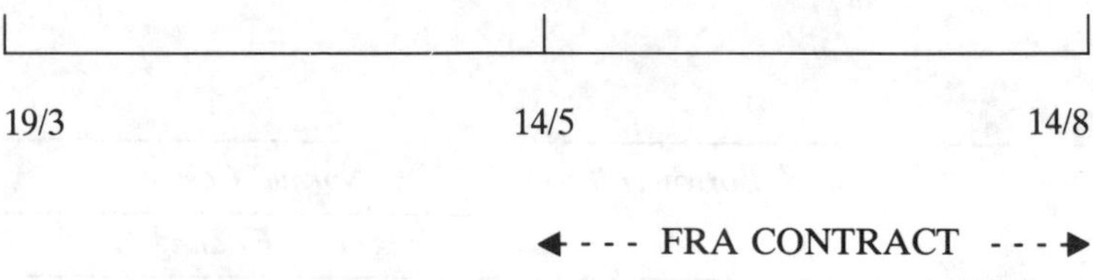

- Borrowing requirement £lm 14/5 → 14/8.
- Customer concern: rates likely to rise.
- Action: purchase FRA contract for which Bank quotes 9.75 per cent for term 14/5 → 14/8.

Settlement

- On 14/5 rates are 11 per cent.
- Bank pays 1.25 per cent x £lm for 92 days.
- Customer borrows in the market at 11 per cent.
- Profit on FRA produces net borrowing at 9.75 per cent.

INTEREST RATE SWAPS

These are agreements by which two parties agree to pay each other interest on a notional amount over a defined period but calculated according to different interest bases. In a simple example, one party would agree to pay interest calculated on a fixed rate basis for the life of the deal and the counterparty would agree to pay interest on a floating rate basis of six-month LIBOR refixed every six months for the life of the deal. At no time is an amount of principal exchanged.

Example

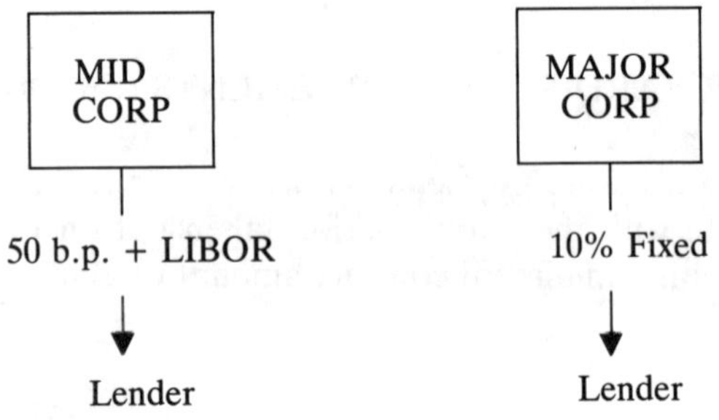

	Borrower Term	Normal Cost	
		Fixed	*Floating*
MID	5 years	12	LIBOR + 50 b.p.
MAJOR	5 years	10	LIBOR

Note: Mid Corp prefers to borrow fixed.
Major Corp prefers to borrow floating.

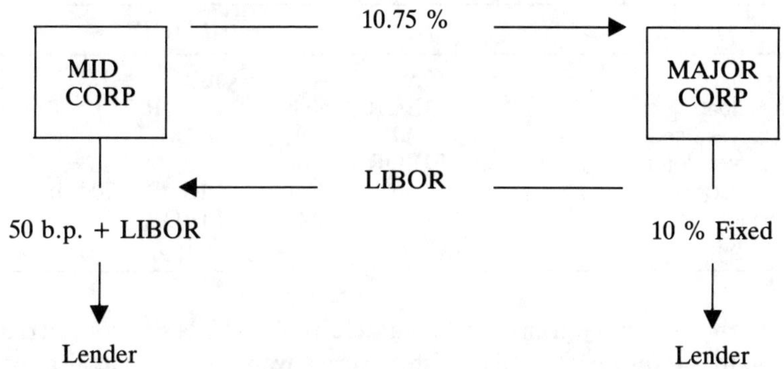

	MID	*MAJOR*
Pays fixed	10.75%	10%
Pays floating	LIBOR + 50 b.p.	LIBOR
Receives fixed	–	10.75%
Receives floating	LIBOR	–
Net cost	11.25%	LIBOR – 75 b.p.
Normal cost	12%	LIBOR
Saving	75 b.p.	75 b.p.

By using the market of comparative advantage both companies improve their margins. However, because it would be very difficult for the two parties to find each other and also the amount of borrowing for each company would undoubtedly be different, a Bank acts as market maker.

Example

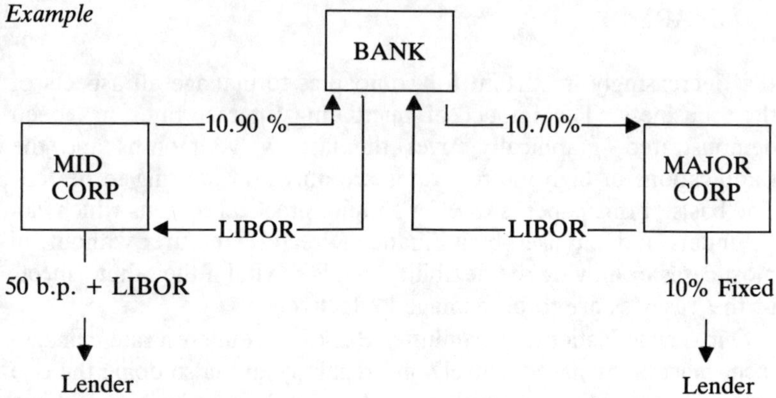

	MID	*MAJOR*
Pays fixed	10.90%	10%
Pays floating	LIBOR + 50 b.p.	LIBOR
Receives fixed	–	10.70%
Receives floating	LIBOR	–
Net cost	11.40%	LIBOR – 70 b.p.
Normal cost	12%	LIBOR
Saving	60 b.p.	70 b.p.

A swap can also be transacted on a deferred start basis ie contracted now for a future start date (stub start swap), or it can also be transacted in line with a cashflow forecast, e.g., phased drawdown/ phased repayment (rollercoaster swap). These are only a few examples of how Swaps can be used

Features

- Amount: minimum £lm, no maximum.
- Term: minimum 2 years, maximum 10 years.

Benefits

- Raise funds at lower interest rates.
- Flexibility.
- Use market of comparative advantage.
- Exercise an interest rate perception.

SUMMARY

It is increasingly important for companies to manage all aspects of their business. The impact of fluctuating interest rates has been demonstrated, graphically, over the last twelve months and the ramifications of high interest rates are only now starting to be felt. The basis of this paper is to offer simple, practical options which can be understood and used by a Finance Director/Treasurer without, in most cases, removing the flexibility that is so vital if the other aspects of the business are to be managed effectively.

Our view at National Westminster Bank is that interest rate management must be managed actively and regularly and in so doing the one remaining variable over which control has in the past been absent can be removed, with consequent improvement in budgeting accuracy.

7 Investment Trust Price Discounts

J. Matatko and Richard Purkis

INTRODUCTION

The 'problem' of the divergence between the market value of shares in a closed-end fund (investment trust) and the valuation of their assets is one that has led to a good deal of research and comment over a period of many years (see the references cited in our second section). The issue has also, perhaps, a broader interest other than simply to those interested in mutual funds. For investment trusts, unlike other companies, there exists a very 'clear' valuation of the company's assets. The difference between the value of these assets and the share price, the former usually being greater than the latter, is clearly quantified. There may well exist large premiums/discounts on the shares of other quoted companies which are much less 'visible' because of the lack of a precise, or even approximately precise, value of their assets. The sharp movement, usually an increase, in the share price of companies being taken over, testifies to a possible wide divergence in asset value and share price. Investment trusts present an opportunity to investigate the movements in this 'discrepancy'. More plainly in an efficient market without frictions the existence of the premium/discount is impossible. Given the presence in the stock market of highly informed and well resourced agents, the existence of a large market information inefficiency is highly unlikely. The most likely explanations have sought to examine the 'frictions' (i.e., transaction costs, market barriers, taxes, etc.) which exist and would impede anyone attempting to realise arbitrage trading profits from the discount/premium. The failure, also, of shareholders to realise one-off gains, in a discount situation, by unitisation (open-ending the fund) requires a sophisticated explanation. Many studies have indeed sought to relate the discount to 'fundamental' factors, without a good deal of success. Others have sought not to 'explain' the discount but to devise trading rules, based on regularities in its movement. In this paper we first survey this previous work and argue that a satisfactory model of the discount/premium level and its time series fluctuation does not yet exist. In our third and fourth sections we present results illustrating the opposite approach to 'fundamental' modelling of the discount. Time series 'Box–Jenkins models' are fitted to discount data and their prediction properties evaluated. A simple trading rule is also examined and some conclusions about the nature of discount movements are presented at the end of the paper.

DISCOUNT EXPLANATIONS

Possible Frictions

Boudreaux (1973), Malkiel (1977), Thomas and Feldman (1976–7) and Woodward and Matatko (1982) have outlined a number of possible reasons for this discount to net asset value.

1. There may be accounting problems in arriving at the net asset value per share, for example, where 'investment letter' shares are held as part of an investment trust's portfolio', the restricted marketability of these investments means that the use of market value for such investments may not be appropriate. Malkiel (1977) has suggested that the true value of shares which have restrictions on their transfer may be only 50 per cent of the quoted market value of non-restricted shares. Similar problems exist for holdings of thinly traded shares, unquoted shares and other venture capital-type investments. If the underlying net asset value of investment trust shares is overstated because of the above factors, then the discount to net asset value will be similarly overstated.
2. The existence of unrealised capital gains within investment trust portfolios means that there is a potential liability to capital gains tax. This may explain part of the discount in countries such as the US where capital gains by investment trust companies are taxable. However, an empirical study by Malkiel (1977) implied in the US that potential capital gains tax could not explain all, or even most, of the discount to net asset value.
3. Management fees and other transaction costs have been suggested as an explanation to the discount to net asset value.
4. Many UK investment trusts are geared. The existence of 'Double Gearing' (i.e., gearing in the underlying portfolio and specific gearing in the investment trust itself) increases the riskiness of the

investment trust shares. The effect of gearing will be to increase the discount when interest rates rise, and vice-versa. The discount will thus be volatile over time.

5. The marketability of the closed-end fund shares themselves has a bearing on the discount. The more marketable the trust, the lower the discount.
6. The performance of the fund managers may affect the discount. Here an inverse relationship between net asset value performance and discount to net asset value is suggested.
7. Naive security market information inefficiency.
8. The distribution policy of the fund has been proposed as a cause of the discount, for example, in the US; where capital gains can be distributed, a high distribution of capital gains lowers the discount to net asset value. Similar arguments have been outlined in relation to income dividend policy.
9. The portfolio sector on geographic disposition, and hence expectations of future capital growth. For example, funds investing in high expected growth areas may trade at a lower discount or premium to net asset value.

Previous Studies

The level of discount to net asset value varies considerably among individual closed-end funds and for the sector as a whole over time. Since the potential gains from successful discount forecasting are considerable, a number of studies have been undertaken to try to 'explain' discounts by fundamental factors. These studies include Malkiel (for the US), and Woodward and Matatko (for the UK).

In a US study, Malkiel performed cross-sectional regressions over an eight-year period from 1967 to 1974 on 24 major closed-end funds. Discounts at year-end were regressed against the following variables:

1. The percentage of unrealised capital appreciation within the fund (*UN*).
2. Distribution policy (average payout of capital gains over the previous five years) (*D*).
3. Proportion of asset value in restricted (letter) stock (*R*).
4. Whether the fund was invested in foreign stocks (*F*).
5. Fund performance.
6. Portfolio turnover.
7. Management fee.

Some variables were highly correlated, such as 1 and 2 above and were not included in the regression together. Malkiel's results were that the (*UN*) coefficient was not always significant. The value had an average of 0.2 and it turned negative in 1973 and 1974. There was a stronger effect with (*R*). The coefficient was highly significant in 1969–74 and averaged just over 0.5 during the total eight-year period, implying that restricted stock was valued by the market at only about 50 per cent of its book value. The coefficient for (*F*) had inconsistent signs and was insignificant in most years. By replacing (*UN*) with (*D*) higher coefficients of determination and *T*-values were obtained. Additionally a performance measure was added to the regressions. It was expected that good risk adjusted performance would be associated with lower discounts; however, the sign varied and was not significant. Finally, the measures of turnover and expense ratios were never found to be significant.

Malkiel also performed a time series analysis of changes in average fund discounts for 1965–72. Three types of variable were used to explain changes in fund discounts:

1. Net redemptions of open-ended fund units were used as a proxy for investor sentiment regarding investment companies.
2. The relationship between changes in the level of discount and changes in the level of Standard and Poor's 500 Index (S & P 500).
3. A dummy variable was added to reflect the fact that in 1970 a major brokerage firm began underwriting and actively selling open-ended fund units where previously it has concentrated on closed-end fund shares.

The results showed that an increase in net redemptions of open-ended funds was associated with an increase in the discount, although the coefficient was not significant. Also, an increase in the S&P 500 was associated with an increase in the level of discounts, and vice-versa (this appears to be the opposite of the UK experience, presumably because UK closed-end funds are more highly geared). A third finding was that discounts tended to widen in 1970 when a major broker reduced sales support to closed-end funds.

In his conclusion, Malkiel thought that only part of the discount could be explained by rational explanations. He thought that it was also important to recognise that the structural equations explaining fund discounts varied over time and so 'market psychology' had an important bearing on the level and structure of discounts. A further explanation Malkiel proposed was independent of the state of the market. On average, closed-end funds are bought at discounts because they are bought through regular brokers who don't like selling them because they receive a much lower commission than on selling open-ended funds. Malkiel's final observation was that since, in the US, the discount narrowed as the market fell, this negative covariance of fund discounts with market movements suggested that closed-end funds should be particularly attractive investments since beta was less than one yet there was no corresponding reduction in long-term return. Malkiel viewed this phenomenon as an imperfection in the valuations of capital assets.

Woodward and Matatko, whose data on 22 closed-end funds in the UK ran from 1968 to 1977, used 15 fundamental factors within the following general sets of factors to explain cross-sectional discount variation:

1. Geographical spread of investments.
2. Marketability of trust shares.
3. Dividend yield.
4. Management expenses.
5. Gearing.

The findings of this study were that the 'optional' linear discount model varied considerably from year to year with no two years having the same set of explanatory variables. Even the factors which were found to be consistently relevant over a number of years examined had estimated coefficients which varied considerably from year to year. The authors concluded that those results indicated that a fundamental analysis of the behaviour of discounts was unlikely to arrive at a forecasting equation which was stable enough for any investor to use in predicting future discount levels.

Trading Rules

A significant amount of empirical work has also been done to test whether abnormal profits can be made from, for example, investing in closed end funds with a high discount to net asset value.

1. Thompson (1978) found that during the period 1940–75, discounted closed-end fund shares adjusted for risk out-performed the market. Also, fund shares standing at a premium were bad

investments during this period. These findings were not consistent with either the two-factor CAPM or market efficiency.

2. Brauer (1984) found that the potential for open-ending a closed-end fund was a function of discount to net asset value. The discounts to net asset value of funds which became open-ended was larger than the discount to net asset value of all funds. Also, overall, the management expenses of closed-end funds were greater than the management expenses of open-ended funds. Management expenses were lower for 'friendly' open-endings than 'hostile' open-endings. Additionally, gains could still be made by investing in closed-end shares on announcement of open-ending and holding for three months.
3. Brickley and Schallheim (1985) found that substantial gains accrued to the shareholders of closed-end funds which open-ended. Funds which become open-ended tend to have higher discounts than non-open-ended funds. Again, significant abnormal returns can be made by investing in closed-end shares on announcement of open-ending, although due to the uncertainty of when the open-ending will finally be completed, risks may be higher. Also, pickings may not be so rich in future as the market has now seen a number of open-endings, and is more able to assess the outcome of future such strategies.
4. Anderson (1986) found successful trading strategies for investing in closed-ended trusts (for example, buy on 20 per cent discount to net asset value, sell on 15 per cent discount to net asset value). Returns for a variety of trading strategies significantly out-performed the S+P 500 Index.
5. Brauer (1988) developed a model using both the discount to net asset value and 'excess' management expenses to predict open-endings. Portfolios of closed end funds with high discounts to net asset value and low 'excess' expenses out-performed portfolios of pure high discount to net asset value funds and CAPM (note that if expenses were excessive this is a proxy for management resistance to open-ending).

DATA AND METHODOLOGY

In this section we first outline the large authoritative data source on which this study is based and specify the approach taken to producing time series models of individual trust discounts.

Data

The data on which this study is based is taken from the comprehensive database maintained by the Association of Investment Trust Companies. This is a file of share prices, net asset values, distributions, capital changes, updated monthly and covering some 208 publicly traded investment trusts. Since this study is concerned with the *time series* behaviour of share prices and net asset values, the data was screened for missing observations. Many trusts showed at least one share price or net asset value missing from their history. In order to proceed with the study and maintain accuracy of estimation only a limited subset of 38 investment trusts with 'satisfactory' share price and net asset value records was used. Trusts were discarded if either:

1. their record of prices and asset values did not cover the five year period 31 May 1984 to 31 May 1989 or,
2. given a record covering the period defined in 1, the trust has at least one pair of *consecutive* observations missing.

Thus no trust is included with less than 60 observations and/or two or more consecutive observations missed. For the estimation of the time series model below, the missing values were essentially treated as parameters to be estimated along with the other model parameters.

Methodology

The problem of modelling discount fluctuations, which is addressed in this paper, is formulated on three levels:

1. The identification and estimation of a time series model for discount behaviour for each trust.
2. The numerical expansion of forecast with actual values.
3. The evaluation of a trading rule based upon the model's estimated parameters.

Identification and Estimation of an ARMA

In the first step, an autoregressive moving average (ARMA) model (see Box and Jenkins 1970; Nerlove, Grether and Carvalho, 1979; or many others, for expansions and application of these forms of time series models). Since the discount is bounded from above by + 1, the share price is never negative, and a process allowing larger and larger premiums and discounts seems unlikely, the discount process was assumed to be stationary and of the form:

$$D_t = \beta + \sum_{i=1}^{K} \rho_i D_{t-i} + \sum_{i=0}^{n} \alpha_i \epsilon_{t-i}, \ \alpha_o = 1 \qquad (7.1)$$

where D_t is the discount at the end of the month t, ϵ_t is a normally distributed white noise process with

$$E(\epsilon_t) = 0$$
$$E(t_1 t_{t-s}) = \sigma^2 \quad , s = 0$$
$$= 0 \quad , \text{otherwise}$$

The parameters k and n are determined either from inspection of the autocorrelation function or, where necessary, selection between competing models based on the Aikake Information Criterion (1970).

The problem of missing data values was resolved either by excluding trusts from the analysis as described above, or by estimation. Where trusts had sufficient observations and did not miss more than one consecutive observation, the missing observation was estimated using Kalman filtering. If the observation occurred at the beginning of a data series, the series was simply started at the first observed data point. Given these missing values, estimates of the model's parameters β, ϱ_i $(i = 1,)$, α_i $(i = 1, n)$, σ^2 were obtained using maximum likelihood, for each of the 43 trusts.

Forecasting

In order to determine the usefulness and validity of the model, an attempt was made to assess its short-term forecasting power. To this end the final 12 months' discounts were excluded from the estimation procedure described above, and forecast values for each of the 12 months using values estimated by the model were obtained. Since the forecast and data periods do not overlap, this obviously provides a useful check on the model's validity over and above its statistical 'goodness of fit'.

A Simple Trading Rule

The forecasting exercise just described gives some idea of the usefulness of a time series model in predicting discounts; like all statistical analyses, however, it does not address directly the financial relevance of its predictions. In order to gain some idea of the model's ability (or inability) to produce worthwhile profits a simple trading rule, along the lines of the results of Thompson (1978) and Anderson (1986) was developed.

The two studies cited both arrive at the conclusion that apparently profitable trades can be made by buying when the discount on a trust is 'particularly high' and selling when it is 'particularly low'. The main problem with these rules is the derivation of a level above which the trust's discount is considered 'too high' or below which the trust's discount is considered 'too low'. The ARMA model (equation (7.1) above can however be used to imply a long-run stationary value of D_t. We illustrate that here by deriving this value for the case of $k=n=1$ (it is seen below in the most typical case in practice).

If equation (7.1) is solved recursively backwards we obtain:

$$D_t = \beta + \beta \sum_{i=1}^{t-1} \rho^i + \rho^t D_O + \sum_{i=1}^{t-1} \rho^{i=1} (\alpha_i + \rho)\epsilon_{t-1} + \alpha_1\rho^{t-1} \epsilon_O \qquad (7.2)$$

The assumption of stationarity of D requires $\epsilon(\epsilon_t) = 0$ for all t. Since we have also assumption $\epsilon(\epsilon_t \mid \epsilon_{t-1}, \ldots) = 0$ for all t, then:

$$\lim_{t \to \infty} E(D_t \mid D_o, \epsilon_o) = \frac{\beta}{1-\rho} = \bar{D} \text{ (say)} \qquad (7.3)$$

This long-run expected value of the discount is also the implied stationary value of D, if the moving average error term is ignored – i.e., it is the solution of the equation

$$\bar{D} = \beta + \rho\bar{D} \qquad (7.4)$$

A similar long-run expected discount can be derived for other orders of ARMA processes.

Another motivation for the use of equation (7.3) would be the view that the 'true' level of the discount depended on factors such as ownership structure which usually change only slowly, and that observed fluctuations occurred either as a result of 'noise' in net asset value figures or market imperfections. This would correspond to the formulation given in equation (7.4).

A trading rule can then be obtained as follows:

- *buy* when $D_t > \bar{D}$.
- *hold* until $D_t < \bar{D}$.
- *sell* at this point.

A (non-risk-adjusted) comparison of the efficacy of this rule with a buy-and-hold strategy is reported below, together with estimates of D for each trust.

EMPIRICAL RESULTS

In this section we present the results of the estimation, forecasting performance and trading rules just described. The results are all based on the AITC databank, operated by the County Natwest (neither AITC nor County Natwest bears any responsibility for any virus in results expressed in this paper).

ARMA Estimation

For each trust an ARMA specification was chosen, based on prior inspection of the autocorrection function of the discounts themselves. The model specification was subsequently confirmed by examination of the residual autocorrelation function after the model had been fitted. In all cases models, were fitted which yielded residual autocorrelation consistent with 'white noise'.

Table 7.1 lists the model estimates (these estimates use a Kalman filtering technique to solve missing data problems; the number of missing observations is shown in Table 7.1). Summarising Table 7.1, the main features of the results shown are:

(a) *Specifications*
These are of three forms (k, n) = (1,1), (1,0) or (2,0), in order of frequency of occurrence. The presence of the first-order moving average component for 21 trusts indicated that not all information about the future discount is contained in its current value. Knowledge of the last error of estimation will improve the forecast. The presence of the (2,0) specification indicates some relationship between discounts separated by two months. There appears to be little rationalisation of the specification except that it may be due to infrequent trading of either the trust or its assets. The (1,0) is, of course, the simplest specification.

Table 7.1 ARMA estimation
(N = no. of valid observations, M = no. of missing observations)

Trust	*N*	*M*	*ARMA (k,n)*		*AR(1)*	*Constant*	*MA(1)*
Alliance	188	0	(1,1)	0.03	.89	.24	.23
Baillie Gifford Technology	50	0	(1,0)	0.05	.90	.17	–
Baillie Gifford Japan	79	0	(1,0)	0.05	.87	.14	–
Bankers	188	0	(1,0)	0.04	.71	.24	–
British Kidney Patient	67	0	(1,0)	0.05	.87	.15	–
Dundee & London	187	1	(1,1)	0.03	.90	.25	.31
EFM American	188	0	(1,1)	0.04	.87	.22	.24
English & Scottish	176	12	(1,1)	0.04	.91	.22	.23
Foreign & Colonial	188	8	(1,1)	0.03	.93	.24	.20
F&C Smaller Companies	185	3	(1,1)	0.03	.93	.25	.24
First Charlotte Assets	85	0	(1,0)	0.08	.89	.03*	–
Fleming American	188	0	(2,0)	0.04	.69	.24	*AR*(2)=0.69
Fleming Far Eastern	188	0	(1,1)	0.04	.92	.25	.29
Fleming Japanese	188	0	(2,0)	0.04	.70	.22	.21
Fleming Mercantile	176	12	(1,1)	0.04	.89	.25	.24
Fleming Overseas	188	0	(1,0)	0.03	.63	.26	–
Fleming Technology	188	0	(1,1)	0.04	.90	.27	.21
Fleming Universal	188	0	(1,0)	0.03	.79	.27	–
Gartmore American Securities	174	14	(1,1)	0.04	.90	.24	.27
Gartmore European	171	17	(1,1)	0.06	.92	.20	.28
Gartmore Information and Finance	172	16	(1,1)	0.05	.85	.26	.27
Govett Atlantic	188	0	(1,1)	0.04	.93	.22	.30
Govett Oriental	188	0	(1,1)	0.04	.95	.24	.26
Greenfriar	188	0	(1,0)	0.05	.89	.24	–
GT Japan	187	1	(1,1)	0.07	.92	.15	.20
Mid Wynd International	80	0	(1,1)	0.04	.74	.17	.46
Monks	188	0	(1,0)	0.04	.69	.27	–
Moorgate	188	0	(1,1)	0.04	.88	.14	–
Personal Assets	57	0	(1,0)	0.06	.76	.12	–
Precious Metals	81	0	(1,0)	0.06	.72	.12	–
Scottish Mortgage	188	0	(1,1)	0.03	.86	.25	.21
Second Alliance	188	0	(1,0)	0.03	.83	.24	–
Shires	185	3	(2,0)	0.04	.64	.10	*AR*(2)=0.26
TR Australia	188	0	(1,1)	0.05	.87	.24	.22
TR City of London	188	0	(1,1)	0.03	.89	.23	.36
Tribune	182	1	(1,0)	0.04	.78	.25	–
TR Property	188	0	(2,0)	0.03	.63	.24	*AR*(2)=0.28
Witan	188	0	(1,1)	0.04	.87	.27	.28

(b) *Parameter estimates*
Shown in Table 7.1 are the (maximum likelihood) estimates of the autoregressive and moving average parameters. Also shown under the heading 'constant', is the 'long-run' discount value described on p. 121 above. The standard error of the estimates is also presented in Table 7.1. This provides some impression of how 'accurate' the model actually is in predicting the discount series.

As the first order autoregressive parameter, the coefficient of last period's discount is significantly different from, and always less than, unity. Recalling that in the case of a random walk the autoregressive coefficient would not significantly differ from 1,0 (and moving average and other coefficients would be approximately zero), the discount is seen to differ from this simple model. The moving average coefficient is, when included, of the order of 0.2–0.3 and significantly different from zero, again indicating a deviation from random walk of investment trust's discounts.

(c) *Forecasting*
Table 7.2 reports the results of the short-term forecasting exercise undertaken. Data for the last 12 months (June 1988–May 1989) were with held from the estimation process and one-step forecasts for each month were generated from the ARMA models for each trust. To assess the usefulness of the forecasts two summary statistics are quoted:

(1) The average absolute error (AAE) for the 12 forecasts – Table 7.2 shows that 18 AAE are less than 2 per cent (i.e., an approximately 8–10 per cent proportionate error) and 18 between 2 and 3 per cent.
(2) The correct direction of the discount change – one feature of ARMA and other time series models is their ability/inability to pick out the correct direction of changes in the variable being predicted. Here we show the number of times (out of 11 changes in the discount at month ends June 1988–May 1989) that the ARMA predicts correctly, change being defined as increase, decrease or no change to 2 decimal places. For each trial, 11/3 successes would be, on average, achieved by pure chance. Only 12 trusts do, in fact, achieve more than four successful predictions. The short-term forecasting properties of the model in these terms do not appear to be high.

Table 7.2 Results of short-term forecasting

Name	*Average error*	*No. of correct discount changes*
Alliance	0.0138	3
Baillie Gifford Technology	0.0324	7
Baillie Gifford Japan	0.0183	3
Bankers	0.0270	6
British Kidney Patient	0.0247	4
Dundee & London	0.0249	5
EFM American	0.0167	6
English & Scottish	0.0171	3
Foreign & Colonial	0.0118	3
F&C Smaller Companies	0.0201	5
First Charlotte Assets	0.0448	4
Fleming American	0.0203	2
Fleming Far Eastern	0.0272	10
Fleming Japanese	0.0274	4
Fleming Mercantile	0.0082	6
Fleming Overseas	0.0228	4
Fleming Technology	0.0165	4
Fleming Universal	0.0344	4
Gartmore American Securities	0.0195	1
Gartmore European	0.0271	5
Gartmore Information and Finance	0.0296	5
Govett Atlantic	0.0210	4
Govett Oriental	0.0127	3
Greenfriar	0.0198	4
GT Japan	0.0143	5
Mid Wynd International	0.0295	4
Monks	0.0185	1
Moorgate	0.0385	5
Personal Assets	0.0287	4
Precious Metals	0.0339	4
Scottish Mortgage	0.0146	1
Second Alliance	0.0132	4
Shires	0.0138	3

continued on page 126

Table 7.2 continued

Name	*Average error*	*No. of correct discount changes*
TR Australia	0.0293	2
TR City of London	0.0187	5
Tribune	0.0162	4
TR Property	0.0216	3
Witan	0.0126	4

(d) *Trading rules*

Although the model's short-term forecasting performance was not high, experiments were made with trading rules (TR in Table 7.3), similar to those used by Anderson (1986). These are based on simply buying when the discount is considered high, and selling when it is low. No rule is given, however, by Anderson for choosing the appropriate high/low 'trigger points'. Since the idea seems to be that if a trust's discount is above (below) some 'underlying' level, this is a market inefficiency, the rule used in this paper was to buy and hold when the trust's discount was above the 'equilibrium' level reported in the 'constant' column of Table 7.3. Two versions of this rule for different policies when out of the trust are shown in Table 7.3. TR–RF assumes investment is an asset giving a constant 8.2 per cent p.a. (i.e., the 'riskless rate'). TR–RM assumes investment in the FT Actuaries' UK Index for the period 'out' of the trust.

A glance at Table 7.3 makes the superior performance of the Buy-and-Hold (TR–BH) strategy obvious. Only four trusts on a TR–RF strategy and four on a TR–RM basis out-perform TR–BH. The reason is evident from the fact that the index returned only 12.85 per cent over the 12 months. Almost all trusts returned well in excess of this amount. Therefore generally any trading rule taking the investor out of a trust under-performed. A longer performance study might well show different results.

Table 7.3 Trading rule adopted

Trust	*TR–RF*	*TR–RM*	*TR–BH*
Alliance	16.0	19.2	36.7
Baillie Gifford Technology	13.1	15.3	21.6
Baillie Gifford Japan	4.9	4.9	4.9
Bankers	8.2	12.8	40.6
British Kidney Patient	26.2	30.7	13.0
Dundee & London	8.2	12.8	23.7
EFM American	8.2	12.8	29.6
English & Scottish	34.6	36.1	36.2
Foreign & Colonial	17.4	20.3	41.4
F&C Smaller Companies	8.2	12.8	28.1
First Charlotte Assets	8.7	8.7	8.7
Fleming American	28.6	33.6	46.1
Fleming Far Eastern	13.2	17.6	34.1
Fleming Japanese	7.0	11.1	20.6
Fleming Mercantile	13.6	16.4	27.9
Fleming Overseas	8.2	12.8	32.2
Fleming Technology	8.2	12.8	17.2
Fleming Universal	8.2	12.8	32.1
Gartmore American Securities	8.2	12.8	43.8
Gartmore European	34.5	28.8	41.6
Gartmore Information and Financial	18.0	22.6	24.4
Govett Atlantic	11.1	15.0	35.9
Govett Oriental	2.6	6.6	47.3
Greenfriar	14.0	14.0	14.0
GT Japan	10.0	13.5	8.1
Mid Wynd International	31.7	31.7	31.7
Monks	8.2	12.8	38.1
Moorgate	8.2	12.8	28.4
Personal Assets	15.9	15.9	15.9
Precious Metals	–1.0	–1.0	–13.8
Scottish Mortgage	16.5	19.7	31.3
Second Alliance	9.7	13.6	34.4
Shires	8.2	12.8	11.1
TR Australia	8.2	12.8	18.9
TR City of London	8.2	12.8	28.6
Tribune	8.2	12.8	38.4
TR Property	8.2	12.8	–39.4
Witan	15.9	18.7	34.3

CONCLUSION

This study began by noting the difficulties and negative results encountered by many previous researchers investigating discount behaviour. In some respects the results produced here have a similar impact. The trading rules and qualitative forecast properties of the discount for individual trusts left something to be desired; on the other hand, the general concept that the discount level and its fluctuations do not represent a simple market inefficiency and are dependent on more complex phenomena appears reasonable. These latter include such things as the difficulty in achieving control, as opposed to simply owning a number of shares, and are often not directly observable. Discount changes due to these fundamental factors may well be expected usually to be slow and 'evolutionary' in nature. Short-term fluctuations may also occur because of temporary market trading conditions and even measurement 'errors'. A more profitable extension of this study would be to allow the 'long-run expected' discount to 'evolve' and itself depend on fundamentals. It would also be useful in the performance evaluation of the trading strategies to incorporate investing in the investment trust sector as well as the risk-free rate and the market when a trust is sold and prior to repurchase. A longer-run performance evaluation of the simple trading rule derived here might well improve results.

References

Aikake, H. (1970) 'Statistical Predictor Information', *Annals of the Institute of Statistical Mathematics*, 22.

Anderson, S. C. (1986) 'Closed-End Funds Versus Market Efficiency', *Journal of Portfolio Management* (Fall).

Boudreaux, K. J. (1973) 'Discounts and Premiums on Closed-End Mutual Funds: A Study in Valuation', *Journal of Finance*, 28.

Box, G. E. P. and G. M. Jenkins (1970) *Time Series Analysis, Forecasting and Control*, San Francisco: Holden-Day.

Brickley, J. A. and J. S. Schallheim (1985) 'Lifting the Lid on Closed-End Investment Companies: A Case of Abnormal Returns', *Journal of Financial and Quantitative Analysis*, 20.

Brauer, G. A. (1984) '"Open-Ending" Closed-End Funds', *Journal of Financial Economics*, 12.

Brauer, G. A. (1988) 'Closed-End Fund Shares' Abnormal Returns and the Information Content of Discounts and Premiums', *Journal of Finance*, 43.

Malkiel, B. G. (1977) 'The Valuation of Closed-End Investment-Company Shares', *Journal of Finance*, 32.
Nerlove, M., D. M. Grether and J. L. Carvalho (1979) *Analysis of Economic Time Series*, New York: Academic Press.
Thomas, D. E. O'D. and K. S. Feldman (1976–7) 'The Development of a Model to Explain Investment Trust Prices and Discounts – Investment Analysis, 48.
Thompson, R. (1978) 'The Information Content of Discounts and Premiums on Closed-End Fund Shares', *Journal of Financial Economics*, 6.
Woodward, R. S. and J. Matatko (1982) 'Factors Affecting the Behaviour of UK Closed-End Fund Discounts 1968 to 1977', *Journal of Business Finance and Accounting*, 9.

8 New Japanese Index Futures Contracts: A Comparison With US and UK Contracts

Desmond Corner and Toru Takenashi

INTRODUCTION

Recent years have seen the development of a major innovation in the area of financial instruments, namely the use of futures contracts on stock indices. This innovation has gone hand-in-hand with the increasing use of index funds as a strategy in passive portfolio management, well developed during the last decade in the US, and now being taken on board in the UK and Japan. This latter development stems from the revolution in investment management outlined by David Damant in Chapter 1.

MAJOR FUTURES MARKETS

Stock index futures are now traded in many countries, as may be seen in Table 8.1.

Many stock index futures contracts started after the Value Line index futures contract introduced on the KCBT. The Standard and Poor's 500 index (S & P 500) futures contract started on the CME in April 1982, the New York Stock Exchange Composite index (NYSE COMPOSITE) futures contract started on the NYFE in July 1984, and the Major Market index (MMI) futures contract started on the CBOT in August 1985. Other stock futures options were also introduced on a number of other exchanges. However, from Table 8.1, it can be seen that the US market has dominated the world stock index futures markets. There are several reasons for this. First of all, the market capitalisation of underlying stocks in many other markets were smaller when compared with that in the US market. Secondly,

Table 8.1 Future market activity by major indices

Exchange	*Based upon*	*Start*	*Value of contract*	*Volume of contract*
KCBT	Value Line	Feb. 82	$500	505551
CME	S&P500	Apr 82	$500	19044673
NYFE	NYSE COMPO	May 82	$500	2915915
CBT	MMI	May 85	$250	2639887
SFE	ASE	Feb 83	A$10	615934
TFE	TSE300	Jan 84	C$10	10247
LIFFE	FTSE100	May 84	£25	469520
HKFE	Hang Seng	May 86	HK$50	3611329
SIMEX	NK225	Sept 86	¥500	363439

Notes: KCBT: Kansas City Board of Trade; CME: Chicago Mercantile Exchange; NYFE: New York Futures Exchange; CBT: Chicago Board of Trade; SFE: Sydney Futures Exchange; TFE: Toronto Futures Exchange; LIFFE: London International Financial Futures Exchange; HKFE: Hong Kong Futures Exchange; SIMEX: Singapore International Monetary Exchange.

institutional investors have not participated in those markets to the same extent as in the US. Thirdly, the characteristics of underlying stock index do not match the portfolios of institutional investors.

Japan did not introduce standard stock index futures contract until September 1988. Although the NK225 futures contract had already been traded at SIMEX from September 1986, and the OSAKA50 had been traded at the OSE since June 1987, the equivalent value of trading volume of contracts was small, only 2.5 per cent and 10 per cent of that of the TSE respectively at October 1987.

In September 1988, two popular standard stock index futures contracts, TOPIX and NK225 contracts, were introduced on the TSE and the OSE respectively. On the other hand, a bond futures contract had already been introduced on the TSE in October 1985, and the equivalent value of trading volume is as big as that of underlying bond markets. Considering the recent trend towards institutionalisation in Japan and the increasing need for the instrument of hedging a portfolio against the market after the October crash in 1987, rapid growth of these stock index futures markets is to be expected.

In terms of the use of stock index futures contracts in passive portfolio management and portfolio insurance within the area of international portfolios, it is particularly important to consider their role in the world's most important stock markets, namely Tokyo, New York and London. Between them, these three financial markets accounted for 83.1 per cent of the market capitalisation of equities comprising the FT Actuaries' (FTA) World index at the end of July 1989.[1] Any passive strategy employed for the construction of an international portfolio must inevitably take these weightings into account. In addition, the managers of internationally orientated passive funds have been increasingly conscious of the need to consider whether they should undertake any form of portfolio insurance to guard against adverse overall market movements. This paper will concentrate particularly on the development and use of index futures contracts in the world's largest equity market, namely Japan, which accounted for 42 per cent of the valuation of the FTA World index at the end of July 1989.[2] In particular, it will consider the growth in the volume of index futures contracts, market trading hours, trading margins and price move limits, commission rates and the characteristics of the underlying stock indices which may affect fund managers' choice of stock futures contracts within the context of program trading and portfolio insurance.

THE GROWTH OF FUTURES MARKET

The volume of trading in futures contracts is very large. In 1987, total trading activity on futures market was over 200m contracts. Of this volume, the debt instruments such as Treasury bonds (T-bonds), notes, bills and Eurodollars accounted for over 40 per cent. However, T-bonds contracts accounted for about three-quarters of this. The total activity on stock index futures markets accounted for 12 per cent of the futures market. But the equivalent value of trading volume of the S & P500 contract was larger than that of the underlying NYSE market in the US. The dollar size of trading volume in the S&P500 contract has exceeded that on the NYSE since the last quarter of 1983, and was about twice as large as that of the NYSE by 1987 (see Table 8.2).

Unfortunately, despite the fact that many stock index futures contracts are traded all over the world, the volume of trading contracts is concentrated on the S&P500 contracts as shown in Table 8.2. Even in the US market, the volume of S&P500 contracts in 1987 had more than doubled its 1983 level, while that of the Value Line and NYSE COMPOSITE contracts decreased. This can partly be ex-

Table 8.2 Futures activity: volume of trading contracts

Exchange	*Based upon*	*1982*	*1983*	*1984*	*1985*	*1986*	*1987*
KCBT	Value Line	528743	724979	910956	1204656	953985	505551
CME	S&P500	2935532	8101687	12363592	15055955	19505273	19044673
NYFE	NYSE COMPO	1432913	3506439	3456789	2833614	3123668	2915915
CBT	MMI				442091	1738916	2630887
SFE	ASE		180014	237011	284148	464475	615935
TFE	TSE300			19014	25050	48490	10247
LIFFE	FTSE100			73590	89308	162511	469520
HKFE	Hang Seng					825279	3611329
SIMEX	NK225					33593	363439

Note: KCBT, etc.: see Table 8.1

plained by the characteristics of each underlying index. In general, the principal need for stock index futures contracts is to hedge portfolios against market risk. Thus, to meet its needs the underlying stock index should reflect stock market price movements as a whole and be based on as many stocks as possible; and the index should not be easily moved by the movement of a specific stock. Moreover, the method of calculation should be both simple and rational, to allow index levels to be registered quickly.

From this point of view, there are some differences between underlying indices in the US. Although the S&P500 index is less popular than the Dow Jones Industrial Average Index, the S&P500 is based on the market value of 500 stocks, which are well diversified across the US market. Hence, the S&P500 futures contract is well suited for use as the instrument to hedge diversified portfolios against market risk. Moreover, institutional investors prefer the S&P index as the benchmark for a portfolio's performance measurement. Other index futures contracts in the US have special features, but they have been used little by institutional investors for portfolio management. The Value Line index is based on approximately 1700 stocks covered by Value Line, computed by taking the geometric mean of the underlying stocks. Almost 90 per cent of these stocks are chosen from NYSE; however, some stocks from other markets are also included. This index seems to differ widely from the market portfolio, and it is very hard to engage in portfolio matching by using this index due to the calculation method employed.

MMI is based on the average price of twenty blue chips. This suits an arbitrage strategy between the actual portfolio which involves exactly the same twenty stocks as the index and an MMI futures contract. However, since the stocks are weighted according to their market price, the index is affected by the movement of highly priced stocks. The number of stocks involved is also much smaller than the number available in the market. Hence, differences between MMI and most managed portfolios occur, especially when small stocks or highly priced stocks move actively. We can say that the characteristics of the underlying stock index are an important factor in the growth of stock index futures markets.

MARKET TRADING SYSTEMS FOR STOCK INDEX FUTURES

US[3]

Financial futures contracts were first traded on the International Monetary Market (IMM) of the CME in 1972, but these related to commodity futures contracts. Trading in stock index futures contracts proper did not take place until 1982, with the contracts on the S&P's 500 stocks Composite index, although futures contracts on US Treasury bonds had been traded since August 1977. These were followed by trading in Treasury notes futures (May 1982), municipal bonds (June 1985), and GNMA-CS contracts (May 1985). In fact, the first market where index futures contracts were traded in the US was on the KCBT in February 1982. This contract was made on the Value Line Average index. A list of all index futures contracts traded on US markets is given in Table 8.3.

It will be seen that there are a large number of different stock indices (8 in all) on which futures contracts may be bought and sold. It is thus possible for a US fund manager to choose that stock index contract which most nearly matches the stocks in his/her own portfolio. The volume of contracts traded has grown rapidly. This success has been due largely to the composition of the underlying stocks within each index. We shall return to this important point more fully in a later section of the paper.

A feature of the US stock index futures contract market is that almost all buyers close their long positions by selling the contract before it matures rather than taking actual delivery. Settlement is by cash only. In order to facilitate transactions of a hedging nature between the different indices, all stock market index futures have the

Table 8.3 Index futures contracts in US

Stock index	*Opening date*	*Market*
Value Line Average	Feb. 1982	KCBT
S&P500	Apr 1982	CME
NYSE COMPO	May 1982	NYFE
S&P100	Jul 1983	CME
Mini Value Line Average	Jul 1983	KCBT
MMI	Jul 1984	CBOT
S&POTC250	Oct 1985	CME
NASDAQ 100	Oct 1985	CBOT

Notes:
KCBT, etc.: see Table 8.1; CBOT Chicago Board of Trade.

same four delivery months. These are March, June, September and December. All futures contracts positions are adjusted on a daily basis (i.e., they are 'marked to market'), and payment is then made. The positions at the end of the trading day are compared with that of the previous day's close and a balance struck (e.g., if the index has risen then the long investor receives the cash difference). The contract value is a product of the 'multiple' and the current futures price, where the multiple is the contract size (e.g., 500 contracts for each of the S&P500, the NYSE COMPOSITE, the Value Line index and the Major Market index). If, for example, the S&P index is standing at 600 and there is a multiple of 500, the value of *one* contract is $500 × 600 or $300,000.

Market orders can take a variety of forms. The simplest, but most dangerous from the investor's standpoint, is the 'market order', which is exercised at the best price obtainable once the order has reached the trading floor. Around three-quarters of all index futures transactions are placed in this way. The 'market not held order' has more flexibility with regard to time and price. For program trading fund managers often make use of the 'market on close order', which guarantees a price. Just as in the case of trades in normal stock orders, a fund manager may place limit orders in either a buying or a selling direction. Other normal stock trading orders such as 'stop orders' and 'buy stop orders' are also possible.

UK

Only one stock index futures contract is traded in London. This is the *Financial Times* – Stock Exchange 100 Index (FTSE100 or 'Footsie'), which is traded on the London International Financial Futures Exchange (LIFFE) situated in the old Royal Exchange building. Although LIFFE opened for trading in September 1982, it was not until May 1984 that a stock index futures contract was introduced. This was made possible by the construction of an entirely new share price index consisting of 100 of the most frequently traded stocks which were also the most likely to be found in the portfolios of institutional fund managers. The index had to be sufficiently wide to be representative of movements in the London market as a whole, but also to be capable of rapid and frequent calculation.

Trading in FTSE stock index futures is carried out by placing orders with broking members of LIFFE. Orders are then passed to the member's booth on the trading floor. The order slip contains details relating to the contract-type, delivery month sale or purchase, quantity and price, and is time-stamped. In the trading pit orders are placed by open outcry. Executed orders are returned to the member's office on the order slip and confirmed with the customer. All confirmed trades are dealt with by the Exchange's computerised matching system and published regularly on the trading floor throughout the day. FTSE100 futures contracts are valued at £25 per full index point. With the index based on 1000 = 1 January 1984 the cost of a contract (in 1 September 1989) would be 2407.5 × £25 (or £60,188). As in the case of the NYSE, contract dates are for March, June, September and December expiry/delivery. The last trading day is the last business day in each delivery month and delivery takes place on the first business day after the last trading day. Minimum precé movement (tick size) is 0.05 and £12.50 value.

On 24 August 1989 it was revealed in the *Financial Times* that the stockbroker Citicorp Scrimgeour Vickers was to launch index futures contracts in industry sectors of the UK stock market in September. Scrimgeour intended to create eight sector indices each weighted by market capitalisation. They were to contain all stocks within the FTA sector and the FTSE100 index. The first contracts to be launched were for the Electronics and Telephone Networks, and the Oil and Gas sectors respectively. Delivery months, last trading days and trading hours were to coincide with those of the FTSE100 futures contract traded on LIFFE. Settlement was to be by cash. This was an important innovation for fund managers who would eventually be able to tailor index futures contracts more closely to the composition of the portfolios under their management.

Japan

The TOPIX and NK225 index futures contracts have been traded on the TSE and the OSE respectively. Unlike other stock index futures contracts in the world, neither are traded on the Future or Commodity Exchange, so their trading systems are similar to those of the underlying stocks.

Both futures contracts are traded continuously in an order-book matching system with batch trading at opening, in the same way as the underlying stocks are traded on stock exchanges. Since there is no market-maker who can trade for his own account like specialists in the US, there is no ask–bid spread.

The TOPIX futures contract is traded on Tokyo's automated trading system, (Computer Assisted Order Routeing and Execution System (CORES)) in which all underlying stocks are traded, except for the 250 actively traded stocks which trade on the floor. Bond futures contracts are also traded in this way. The advantage of using an automated trading system is that it enables transactions to be traded quickly, because the price and volume transacted are automatically revised and then provided through the Exchange Information System and information services such as QUICK every one minute to meet continuous trading.

There is criticism that Japanese order-book matching system is much 'thinner' than the NYSE's specialist trading system, because no one is expected to buy or sell for his own account to offset order imbalances. Therefore, Japanese exchange uses a 'Price-Move Limits' system to supply enough liquidity for trading order imbalances under strong pressure, as in the panic in the October crash in 1987.

However, there are some special days when order imbalances tend to occur, even where there is no panic. These are expiration days. In the US, it is well known that futures contracts increase market volatility, both of futures and of underlying stocks, on the expiration day of futures contract. In particular in the last one hour up to expiration, indices tend to fall or rise substantially. Franklin R. Edwards (1988) presented statistical evidence that indicated that there had been unusual volatility at the expiration of the S&P500 futures contracts based on data between July 1983 to October 1986. The standard deviation of the return on the Options or Futures expiration day is significantly greater than normal days at the 5 per cent level of significance, and from 3 p.m. to close on expiration day is significantly larger than normal days at the 5 per cent level. Such volatility occurs when an arbitrageur, who had a long (or short) position in the futures contract and sold (or bought) stocks in the index, uses a market at close order to buy (or sell) a basket of stocks, while holding the contract to expiration. Such 'trades at close' tend to cause imbalances between demand and supply of stocks, and lead to sharp price movements.

The attraction to investors of these transactions is due to the cash settlement feature of stock index futures contracts. Since the price of the futures contract is replaced by the index value at the expiration, we can eliminate any basic risk associated with closing our positions. Moreover, we can offset the market impact of large volume trading between futures and underlying index, because both prices are coincident at expiration. This is very attractive even if we are not arbitrageurs. Suppose we have to invest a considerable amount of money in an index fund. In general, there are market impacts in such an investment. However, we can offset market impacts by buying futures contracts just before expiration and buying underlying stocks using market-at-close orders. The commission and market impacts of futures contracts are very small, and we can easily construct a portfolio in a short time.

In contrast to TOPIX the OSAKA50 provides for security delivery. Its settlement price at expiration is the closing price of futures contracts rather than the index value. This is because settlement could not take place solely in cash due to the rule which was made at the end of the second World War.

TRADING HOURS

From the fund manager's standpoint trading hours for index contracts are of considerable importance when it comes to opening and closing positions with a view to portfolio insurance techniques. Typical trading hours are shown in Table 8.4.

There are special trading hours for the last trading day, generally organised so as to fit in with the hours of opening of the exchanges on which the securities contained within each index are listed.

Trading hours of TOPIX and NK225 are divided into two sessions:

Table 8.4 Trading hours for major stock index futures contracts

	Index contract	*Trading hours**
US	S&P500	9.30–16.15 EST
	NYSE COMPO	9.30–16.15 EST
	MMI	9.15–16.15 EST
	Value Line	9.30–16.15 EST
London	(LIFFE)	
	FTSE100	9.05–16.05
Japan	(TFFE)	
	TOPIX	9.00–11.15 JST 12.30–15.15 JST
	Osaka	
	NK225	9.00–11.15 JST 13.30–15.15 JST

Notes:
* Local times.
TFFE Tokyo Financial Futures Exchange.

from 9.00 to 11.15 and from 12.30 to 15.[4] Each period is fifteen minutes longer than that of the underlying stocks so that investors or dealers can adjust their futures position according to the final closing price of the index value. However, trading hours are limited until 15.00 on the final trading day, because the futures price is replaced by the closing price of the index at 15.00. This system is not used by S&P500 and NYFE COMPOSITE, because their settlement prices are the special quotations made by using the opening price of index stocks one working day after the final trading day. To reduce expiration-day volatility, the settlement time of these indices is different from those of the MMI and Value Line contracts.

SETTLEMENT PROCEDURES

Futures trading requires both standardised contracts and a centralised settlement system for its efficient operation; official clearing systems developed as a guarantee of the financial integrity of the futures and options markets. As mentioned earlier, the clearing organisations enable all gains and losses to be settled daily.

Most US clearing houses are organised separately from the exchanges which they serve. However, of the above, the CME Clearing

Table 8.5 Settlement procedures organisations

	Exchange	*Clearing organiation*
USA	CBT	Board of Trade Clearing Corporation
	CME	Chicago Mercantile Exchange Clearing House
	NYFE	New York Futures Clearing Corporation
	KCBT	Gain Clearing Corporation
UK	LIFFE	International Commodities Clearing House (ICCH)
JAPAN	TSE/TFFE	Japan Securities Clearing Corporation
	OSE	Japan Securities Clearing Corporation

Notes: CBT, etc.: see Table 8.1; OSE Osana Stock Exchange; TSE Tokyo Stock Exchange.

House is an exception and acts as a department of the exchange. In each case, the clearing corporation places itself between buyer and seller and vice-versa, and is looked upon for payment. This situation arises because futures contracts are sold with no deposit. (Margin requirements are discussed in the following section.) The clearing house also acts in an agency capacity, providing a mechanism whereby sellers of contracts are able to make delivery to purchasers. In general, both rules and procedures are determined by each individual clearing house. In London, clearing is done via the ICCH, a body completely separate from LIFFE markets, whilst in Japan clearing is done via the Japan Securities Clearing Corporation which is a subsidiary of the TSE. Final settlement of TOPIX and NK225 takes place in cash rather than by delivery of securities, like other stock index futures contracts. Both contracts are marked to market on the expiration day, with the final futures price replaced by the underlying stock index value.

Both contracts have the settlement dates on every 10th day of four contract months such as March, June, September and December (if it is a holiday, the next working day is used). The settlement day of the 10th of the month is earlier than the third Friday of US futures contracts, because it is based on the fact that the 10th is easy to remember, and it does not overlap with the ex-dividend day of underlying stocks in Japan because this is not used as an xd date.

Another difference is the last trading day; it is three working days before the settlement date. It takes four days until settlement is

Table 8.6 Settlement systems

	Contracts			
	US		*UK*	*Japan*
	S&P500 *NYFE COMPO*	*Value Line* *MMI*	*FTSE100*	*TOPIX NK225*
1. Last trading day	One trading before third Friday of contract	Third Friday of contract month	Last trading day in delivery month	Three working days before settlement
2. Settlement day	Next working day of third Friday of contract month	Next working day of third Friday of contract month	Daily	10th or next working day of contract month
3. Settlement price	Special quotation of opening price of index at third Friday	Closing price of index at last trading day	Based on average level of FTSE100 between 11.10 and 11.20 on last trading day	Closing price of index at close of session of last day
4. Contract Month	March, June, September, and December	March, June, September, and December	March, June, September, and December	March, June, September, and December

completed, three days longer than in the case of US contracts.

Both contracts use the closing level of their index value as the settlement price. Therefore, market at close orders may concentrate at the closing on last trading days. If such unusual volatility continues to be found, stock exchanges may change one of their settlement prices to the opening price of the next day to diversify orders like the S&P500 and NYFE COMPOSITE contracts.

Details of the various settlements systems are given in Table 8.6.

PRICE MOVE LIMITS

Although there are minimum price investments for index futures contracts in both the US and the UK (tick size and value) price move limits are more particularly a Japanese phenomenon.

Price move limits prohibit trading outside the limits for the remainder of the trading day. Once the limits are reached, the Exchange

Table 8.7 Price move limits in US and Japan

	S&P500 *Value Line*	*NYSE* *COMPO*	*MMI*	*TOPIX* *NK225*
	$X \overset{\text{def}}{=}$ index value of S&P500	25 points	20 points	About 3%*
Limit	$X >= 325 => \text{limit} = 25$ $325 > X >= 275 => 20$ $X < 275$ 15 Until 10 min after opening => limit = 5	Expand to 35 after two days of limit moves	Expand to 30 after two days of limit moves	

Note:
* See text below.

halts the trading until the next day. Table 8.7 indicates price move limits in the US and Japan.

Price move limits attempt to maintain a market to adjust calmly to quick-moving prices, promoting acceptable liquidity. They help to protect participants from unexpected heavy loss exposure due to unlimited price movement.

On 23 October 1987, after a substantial decline of markets during the week, the 30 point price move limits on the S&P500, equivalent to a 12 per cent move, were instituted by the CME. The only times in the history of the S&P500 in which a move of more than 12 per cent was experienced were on 19 and 22 October 1981. In response to the CME, other futures exchanges also imposed price move limits. The NYFE and the KCBT imposed on NYSE COMPOSITE and Value Line index futures contracts limits of 25 and 30 points, respectively. The CBT implemented 40 points limits for MMI on 13 January 1988. However, no such a magnitude of movement has occurred since then. The above exchanges have now narrowed their price limits.

About 3 per cent price move limits are imposed on TOPIX and NK225 contracts. It is not possible to be more specific because the actual percentage also depends on the level of values. This 3 per cent is smaller than the 5–7 per cent of the S&P500 contract. This is partly explained by the difference of view between US and Japanese authorities. The SEC believes that there are substantial problems with price move limits' effectiveness, because price declines in the stock market after futures hit the price limits would place futures traders at substantial risk due to the inability to adjust their futures positions. Conversely, the TSE believes that the price limits protect investors from unexpected damage due to abrupt price movement. This is due to the special situation in Tokyo where the dominance of four broker–dealers (Nomura, Nikko, Yamaichi and Daiwa), coupled with longer stock-holding periods on the part of both individuals and corporations, may support and stabilise markets.

Price move limits are also imposed on underlying stocks in Japanese markets. However, they are more than 10 per cent for cash stock. If all stocks move in the same direction (as in the October crash), and futures prices reach the price move limits, while the underlying stock index moves still further beyond the futures price move limits, emergency action can be taken. Hence price move limits can be controlled by the stock exchange. If the spread between the futures contract and underlying index widens so far that the futures market loses its function, these limits can be expanded.

This also involves a trade-off between liquidity and safety. As the futures contracts approach the limits, investors may drive the price even further towards the limits, or may drive the price back from the limits, afraid of being locked into their position. In either case, the limits seem to act as a psychological wall. The higher level of price move limits provides a large liquidity and trading opportunity. However, investors suffer from the possibility of damage in highly volatile markets, especially when they are acting in panic. Whilst the lower level of price move limits protects investors, it may act as a psychological wall: unwilling to have the risk of holding their position overnight, investors suffer from low liquidity.

Although we cannot distinguish between a panic reaction and a fundamentally justified price change, a move of more than 10 per cent market index in a day should be unusual. Price move limits would have to be imposed on at least either futures or stocks, because the existence of a substantial futures price discount discouraged specialists and other market participants from offsetting order imbalances in the US crash. In Japan, investors were forced to accept the risk of holding their position overnight, while the limits protected investors who might have sold below the price move limits. And, perhaps, price move limits are particularly important for 'thin' markets. We found a typical example in the trading of the NK225 contract on SIMEX. The NK225 contract opened at the price of about one-fifth of the index value of the previous day in the October crash. Although this is an extreme, we must recognise the possibility of unusual action under panic conditions.

TRANSACTIONS COSTS AND MARGIN REQUIREMENTS

US

Just as commission rates on the purchase and sale of stocks have been negotiable since May Day 1975, so too are those on stock index futures. Such commissions are based on a round trip. For institutional investors the typical commission per contract was around $15 at the end of the 1980s.

Provided that the premium has been paid in full, there are no margin requirements for the buyer of an index futures contract. However, in cases where the premium has not been paid in full, then the traditional margin requirements of each stock exchange must be met. There is also a variation margin which occurs with the daily gains/losses in connection with the marked to market position. Daily adjustments must be made in respect of changes in contract value. The margin requirements include both an initial margin and a maintenance margin. In the former case this is the minimum amount which a purchaser must pay before a transaction takes place. Maintenance is a top-up concept so that positions may be maintained. Initial margins in the US are determined by the Federal Reserve Board, the SEC and the relevant exchange. Broking firms may also set their own margin requirements.

Margin requirements differ according to whether the contract is taken out by hedgers, speculator or spreaders. In the case of index futures there is a fixed dollar amount which may be adjusted from time to time to take account of the changes in the stock index level. Table 8.8 sets out the position with regard to hedgers in each of the three countries.

UK

Commission rates became fully negotiable on 26 October 1986 (see Table 8.9).

All users of LIFFE, whether buyers or sellers, are required to put up margins. These funds are held by the Clearing House. The

Table 8.8 Stock index futures margins requirements for hedgers

	US COMPO				*UK*	*Japan*	
Contract:	*S&P500* ($)	*NYSE COMPO* ($)	*XMI* ($)	*Value Line* ($)	*FTSE 100* (£)	*Nikkei*	*TOPIX*
Initial	10000	5000	10000	3000	3000	Minimum $6m 9% of contract value (3% in cash)	
Maintenance	10000	5000	10000	3000	3000	6%	

Table 8.9 Commission rates

Yen value of TOPIX and NK225 contracts – 0.1bn %	*0.1–0.3 bn %*	*0.3–0.5bn %*	*0.5–1bn %*	*1bn*
0.4	0.03	0.02	0.01	0.005

minimum (initial) level is set by the Clearing House and reflects the volatility of the stock index (FTSE100). Consequently the value of outstanding contracts will change and a 'variation' (maintenance) margin is added to or subtracted from each margin account. In order to maintain an initial margin, cash must be added to the account if the value of the contract increases on changes in the underlying index.

Commissions are much lower than those on underlying stocks. They are fixed by the exchange according to the yen value of trading contracts. Suppose the NK225 is traded at ¥30,000 and we have a long position of ¥0.4bn equivalent value of contract, the commission is 0.02 per cent or ¥6 for each ¥30,000, which is less than ¥10 (the value of 'tick') (i.e., the minimum unit value of the price move). Futures commission can therefore be negligible compared with other transaction costs.

Japan

The futures contracts generally offer financial leverage. The capital investment is low compared with the underlying asset, and even less than the margin requirement in stocks, because futures margins differ from stock margins in concept. Futures margins are performance bonds and do not involve an extension of credit.

A commission of capital investment required can be made as follows.

A trading lot of the TOPIX contract is the index times ¥10,000, and that of the NK225 futures contract is the index times ¥000, and that of the S&P500 futures contract is the index times $500. Suppose the TOPIX, the NK225 and the S&P500 futures contracts are traded, at roughly 2,400, 30,000 and 300 respectively, the approximate value of them is ¥24 m (or $0.18m), ¥30 m (or $0.23m), and $0.15 m ¥ respectively.

On the other hand, the initial speculative margins required as capital investment for TOPIX and NK225 contracts are only 9 per cent compared with 12 per cent of S&P500 contract (18,000/15,000 = 12 per cent). The approximate value of margin required by the TOPIX, the NK225 and the S&P500 are $16,200, $20,700 and $18,000 respectively. Moreover, fund managers can use underlying stocks as a substitute for the margin required by the TOPIX and the NK225 up to 3 per cent. As a result, only 6 per cent of cash is required.

Although the minimum margins required by Japanese exchanges are in percentage forms rather than in actual amounts, both the TOPIX and the NK255 contracts are designed to provide more leverage for investors compared with the US contracts. These minimum standing levels of margins are usually set by the exchange; however, brokers are permitted to set higher margins to customers than the minimum required.

In general, margin requirements depend on the variability of underlying assets, the margin being raised above normal levels during times of high variability.

For example in the US, during the October 1987 crash, the S&P500's margin was raised in a series of steps to $20,000 ($15,000 for hedgers) from $10,000 ($5,000 for hedgers). In December, however, its margin levels were reduced to $15,000 ($10,000 for hedgers), and in September 1989 an investor needed only approximately 12 per cent of the contract value (8 per cent for hedgers). Nevertheless, these margins are much lower than the 50 per cent margin requirement for investors in stocks.

In Japan, the margin requirement in stocks is more than 30 per cent. However, it is usually from 50 per cent to 70 per cent – that is, much higher than the 9 per cent margin needed on futures. There is obviously a trade-off relationship between liquidity and safety of investors. The lower the margin, the easier it is for investors to take positions and the greater is the liquidity. The impact of current low margin levels is that an institutional investor can use the stock index futures contract to establish a long position or short position quickly with a margin deposit of about one-tenth of the stock equivalent position.

Changing the margin rate means that the value of futures contract is changed in terms of the power to control underlying stocks. The lower the margin, the greater the power of control. However, low margins contribute to speculative trading, which under normal market conditions contributes to the illusion of almost unlimited liquidity in futures markets. But in the US, during the October crash, this unlimited liquidity turned out to be only an illusion, because the persistent discounts that appeared in the S&P500 futures contract on 16 October, and continued at record levels on 19 October and throughout that week, prevented investors from selling the index futures contract. The enormous discounts between the futures contract and the underlying stocks index indicated that the market was going to decline and thus buyers waited until stocks declined to even lower levels.

As discussed before, the CME increased the margin requirement during the market break. However, the TSE decreased the margin required in stocks from 70 per cent to 50 per cent immediately after the market break to supply liquidity. This partly explains the fact that the Japanese market stopped going down and recovered relatively earlier than the US market.

CHARACTERISTICS OF THE UNDERLYING INDICES

Underlying indices are very important for the growth of futures markets. Fund managers will wish to use stock index futures contracts for hedging purposes, particularly in cases where a passive approach to portfolio management is being used. In this case, a broadly-based index is the most suitable for mirroring market movements; but there are bound to be tracking errors even with a widely-based portfolio. Although various indices may mirror each other and the market over long periods of time, fund managers' needs are best served by those indices which match their own requirements. This is particularly the case where a fund manager is following a rather more active policy, but nevertheless wishes to hedge against a large movement in the market. The major characteristics of the underlying indices are shown in Table 8.10.

US

The US fund manager has a much wider choice in the use of indices than his colleague in either Japan or the UK. The manager who wishes to use an index futures contract for protecting a passive portfolio, or that part of a large pension fund's portfolio which is being managed in a passive fashion, may choose between the SP500 contract or the NYSE COMPOSITE contract. For long-term purposes both will be subject to market tracking errors because of the lack of inclusion of a sufficient number of small/medium-size stocks within the index. The extent of divergence also depends on weighting methods and type of mean calculated.

UK

The FTSE100 was devised alongside the introduction of index futures contracts. Despite the fact that it consists of just 100 α stocks, the index coverage accounts for around 70 per cent of total market capitalisation. From the standpoint of the fund manager carrying out a passive portfolio policy for a UK general fund, it is deficient in its inclusion of small companies, but will nevertheless enable the fund manager to cover around two-thirds of the value of such a portfolio.

Japan

Two different contract-related indices started on the same day in Japan. Investors chose between these indices according to their needs. Since the major part of trading systems are the same between them, characteristics of both indices must be very important factor to the growth of their markets.

TOPIX

TOPIX has been calculated since July 1989. It was adjusted by the value of market capitalisation at 4 January 1968 so that it was equivalent to 100. And it is based on the total outstanding of Tokyo Stock Exchange section 1 (TSE1).

Table 8.10 Characteristics of stock indices underlying stock index futures contracts

Index characteristics	*US*			*UK*	*Japan*	
	SP 500	*NYSE Compo*	*Value Line*	*FTSE*	*Nikkei*	*TOPIX*
Numbers of securities and characteristics	500 Mostly NYSE & some AMEX & OTC	ALL NYSE stocks	1700	100	225	All section 1 stocks 1101
Adequate representation of small market capitalisation stocks	No	No	No	No	No	No
Weighting characteristics	Value weighted	Value weighted	Equal weighting, constant re allocation	Value weighted, reallocated quarterly	Equal weighting, constant re allocation	Value weighted
Calculation method	AM	AM	GM	AM	GM	AM
Base date	1941–3 = 100	31 Dec. 1965 = 50	30 Jun. 1961 = 100	1 Jan. 1984 = 100	21.43 divisor factor 31 Dec. 1986	4 Jan. 1968 = 100
Dividends included	No	No	No	No	No	No
Adjustment for splits, rights issues, etc.	Yes	Yes	Yes	Yes	Yes	Yes
Stock liquidity	High	Medium	Medium	High	High	High

Advantages of using TOPIX are:

(1) TOPIX reflects the whole market price movements of TSE1 and is considered by investors as close to the market portfolio. It is thus, suitable as the instrument to hedge portfolios against market risk.
(2) TOPIX contains all stocks listed in TSE1 and each stock is weighted according to its capital outstanding. It does not suffer from irregular price movements of small and high priced stocks.

Disadvantages of using TOPIX are:

(1) TOPIX is less popular than NK225 because is started 20 years after NK225.
(2) It is very difficult to manage an actual portfolio which tracks TOPIX. TOPIX involves about 1100 stocks, therefore holding each stock according to its market value needs a large amount of money. Moreover, this portfolio must be adjusted whenever the index is adjusted due to changes such as new issue listing, right issues and delistings.
(3) Financial institutions account for more than 30 per cent of the market capitalisation while their trading volumes are relatively 'thin'. Moreover, their prices were fixed at a face value of ¥500 ten years before due the control of banks. Although they are floated now, their prices are still sometimes controlled.
(4) Although NTT, the largest company in terms of market capitalisation, is listed, the government still owns about 65 per cent of its shares.

NK225

NK225 has been calculated since May 1949. It is a Dow-adjusted price average of 225 typical shares listed on TSE1; simply add up the stock price of all 225 shares to its market price and then divide by the constant divisor.

Advantages of using NK225 are:

(1) Unlike the Dow Jones Industrial Average in the US, NK225 does not change the stocks involved artificially (exceptions exist such as NTT). However, it has been calculated continuously (in principle) since 1945.

(2) NK225 is well known all over the world because of its long history of publication. Most investors, now only individual but also institutional investors, use NK225 when they discuss the Tokyo market.
(3) Managing the actual portfolio which closely tracks NK225 is easier compared with TOPIX. Suppose we construct a portfolio which involves all the 225 stocks and hold 1000 shares each (the minimum lot) the value of the package of stocks is only ¥300 m. Investors can trade this package of shares in the market. The same kind of package for TOPIX is hard to construct. More than ¥5 bn and at least 300 stocks are needed to make such a portfolio which closely tracks TOPIX. For this reason, many NK225 index funds are also managed.
(4) There are some stocks which have less liquidity. Most stocks have been kept in the NK225 for a long time. As a result, some of them become out of date and lose liquidity.
(5) NK225 tends to suffer from high priced stocks' movement. Consider the influence of a 10 per cent rise in shares, one particular share is traded at ¥100 and another is traded at ¥1,000; the latter has ten times as big an impact as the former on the price movement of the index.
(6) There are some small but high priced stocks with a 'thin' trading volume. Hence NK225 has been considered to be more volatile during a day than TOPIX.

SOME INDEX-RELATED STRATEGIES

In conclusion we look at some index-related strategies which may be linked to the use of stock index futures contracts.

Program Trading

Over the last ten years, a number of broker–dealers and large institutional investors have developed computer trading, which means the use of computers for trading techniques and for trading strategies. Equity trading was quite simple before that time; mostly, trading was based on fundamental analysis or technical analysis of individual stocks, and trading was executed for each stock. In the 1960s, at the NYSE, an order received by a broker–dealer's registered representative at a branch office would be telephoned to the firm's order desk; the firm's order desk would in turn telephone the order to the firm's booth on the floor of the NYSE and a firm representative would take the order to the specialist location for the particular stock and execute a trade with either the specialist or other trading interest represented in the crowd. The major evolution of the trading system occurred in 1976, because the rising volume of transactions continued to strain the resources of the firms and NYSE. The NYSE implemented its DOT (Designated Order Turnaround) system in 1976. Initially, DOT was designed to provide a method of by-passing the member firm floor booth for small customer orders. However, it provided a mechanism whereby small market orders could be directly routed from the member firm branch office to the applicable specialist post. The advantage of using DOT for the customer is that it provides very rapid delivery of orders to the exchange floor, and rapid reporting of transacted orders back to the customer. Currently, member firms may route orders of up to 2099 shares through DOT in market and marketable limit orders. Orders are guaranteed execution and reported back to the customer within 3 minutes. DOT also accepts order sizes larger than 2099 shares – up to 30,099 shares – but with no time reporting guarantee.

From the introduction of the DOT system, stocks began to be traded in packages rather than individually. This is partly explained by the institutionalisation in the 1980s. As a result of the increase of total equity holdings, institutional investors have made increasing use of passive asset management strategies, and asset allocation strategies; they have begun to manage index portfolios, and to control their portfolio risk by buying or selling packages of stocks. Moreover, increased use of derivative products such as an index of options and futures has accelerated this so-called program trading. In response to these movements, the NYSE developed the DOT list, which is an application of DOT that allows member firms to send orders through DOT in, as its name implies, a list of securities. DOT list processing enables members to enter large numbers of stocks quickly. With the development of trading strategies parallel to that of techniques, program trading has developed even more fully. Arbitrageurs control the futures and stock markets more efficiently, and institutional investors control their portfolios either by using futures or packages of stocks more effectively.

Since 1982, Tokyo's Second Section trading (dealing in 431 small and medium-size stocks) has been on the fully automated CATS (Computer Assisted Trading System). CATS was extended to all but

Table 8.11 System funds in Japan

	Launch	*Management co.*	*Fund name*	*Management policy*	*Initial asset*
1	25 Dec. 1968	Nomura IT	MIP	NK225 tracking	3
2	20 Sep. 1985	Daiwa IT	Stock Index 225	NK225 tracking	14
3	13 Feb. 1986	Nikko IT	Index Fund TSP	Bara model	13
4	23 May 1986	Yamaich IT	Index Fund 225	NK225 tracking	15
5	8 Oct. 1986	Daiwa IT	Chance '86	RRH model	99
6	27 Mar. 1987	Nomura IT	Dynamic Select	Factor model	93
7	25 May 1987	Nomura IT	System Portfolio	PI	99
8	29 May 1987	Daiwa IT	Stock System '87	PI	00
9	29 Jul. 1987	Nikko IT	System Dynamics	PI	70
10	29 Jul. 1987	Yamaich IT	System Trust '87	PI	90

Note: 1–4 Open type – Additional funds continue to flow into the fund after launch.
5–10 Unit type – No additional funds after launch.
Source: *A Handbook of Investment Trusts* (Tokyo: Nomura IT, 1987).

250 of its First Section in mid-1985. In CATS, the '*saitori*' have no role and orders go directly to the order book in the computer system. The advantage of using this system for the customer is that it provides very rapid delivery and reporting, normally within 5 minutes, and there is no restriction of orders size. However, there are still 250 stocks traded on the floor by '*saitori*'. Perhaps this partly explains the fact that there is less computer trading in Japan than there is in the US, because of the uncertainty of the time reporting guarantee of stocks traded on the floor. In 1985 there was also a boom in index funds. Many investment trusts were launched, as shown in Table 8.11, although the Nomura Investment Trust had already introduced an index tracking fund in 1968. Institutional investors began to use passive management strategies together with the development of trading systems from 1985 onwards.

In contrast to the US DOT list system, Tokyo's CATS does not provide a list processing system; investors have to enter orders one by one. According to the development of new trading strategies such as portfolio insurance and dynamic asset allocation, institutional investors have also developed new trading systems. As shown in Table 8.11, many investment trust management companies launched system funds, whose trading strategies depended on a theoretical rule, such as index tracking, portfolio insurance and other market models. Such funds have increased package trading; for example, Nomura

Table 8.12 Program trading applications

Broker/dealers	
Risk management	Hedge a guaranteed portfolio execution due to increase of program trading
Arbitrage	Index arbitrage between index and futures
Institutions	
Portfolio management	Asset allocation and hedging Portfolio insurance
Index fund management	Investing cash flows and dividends Index arbitrage between index and futures

Table 8.13 Major users of stock index futures contracts in US

	Locals	*Brokerage*	*Individuals*	*Institutions*	*Arbitrageurs*
Volume	50%	12%	5%	18%	15%
Interests	0%	10–25%	5%	25–40%	10–50%
Hedging Time	5 min	15 min–1 hour	A few weeks	A few months	1–3 months

Source: Estimated by Morgan Stanley (1987).

Securities Investment Trust Management Co. developed a package trading system in December 1987, which produces packages of orders automatically and which can quickly be entered into Tokyo's CATS system.

Since September 1988, two stock index futures contracts have been introduced, and a new computer trading system plan, which is named On-line program 4, is in progress. Program trading was expected to become more active in the next stage of development.

Concerning program trading, several important index-related trading strategies have been developed over the past few years for purposes such as those listed in Table 8.12. Stock index futures are particularly important as an instrument for these strategies. The major usage of stock index futures by customer type is shown in Table 8.13; from this, it appears that liquidity is maintained by locals or broker firms, while a hedging strategy is mainly used by institutional investors instead of buying or selling underlying stocks. An arbitrage strategy is mainly used by locals or brokerage firms, and participation of individuals is relatively low. Accordingly, the following sections describe some of the basic strategies such as arbitrage, asset allocation, hedging, portfolio insurance and index fund management.

Portfolio Insurance

Portfolio insurance is a strategy that provides protection against loss at some cost, while still allowing for potential upside gains. Portfolio insurance is usually designed by preset parameters such as the return floor, time horizon and volatility. In its most common form, as implemented with stock index futures contract, a portfolio insurance has an expected cost that depends on assumed volatility over the time horizon. In effect, portfolio insurance comprises a group of methods that attempt to create a long put. In this manner, portfolio insurance is roughly analogous to the use of stop–loss orders in individual securities.

Portfolio insurance can be implemented by using stock index options, stock index futures or stocks as a trading instrument. With stock index options, a stock index plus a stock index put option creates this strategy directly. When using stock or stock index futures for portfolio insurance, the insurer synthesises a long European put by continuously varying the size of the positions in these instruments. Because of the frequent adjustment required by this trading, this is often referred to as 'dynamic hedging' which creates a pay-off pattern that replicates changes in the value of an option. Today, portfolio insurance is usually implemented through dynamic hedging with index futures, because the time frame of listed options contracts does not suit the designed horizon of portfolio insurance, while futures contracts are easy to roll over. In addition, they have relative liquidity, low costs and ease of execution. As stocks prices fluctuate, the proportion of stocks to riskless asset in the portfolio is continuously rebalanced. In effect, as the stock market rises, the size of the hedged portion is reduced by buying stock index futures; as the stock market falls, the size of the hedged portion increases by selling stock index futures. Therefore, as asset values fall to that floor, nothing is invested in stocks, while as asset values increase, the amount invested in stocks increases, reaching the total value of the assets in the upper limit.

The trades of portfolio insurance are, therefore, on the same side as the direction of the market. The disciplined selling in a declining market (or buying in a rising market) of a set amount of futures tends to make futures cheap (or expensive) relative to their theoretical value. This condition tends to induce a substantial arbitrage between stocks and futures. Under these conditions, transactions that would ordinarily be taken in a futures contract would be sent to the stock market. Accordingly, portfolio insurance is implemented through a flexible variety of options, stocks and futures. For example, the chaotic conditions on the futures and securities markets near the close on 16 and 19 October 1987, including persistent discounts of futures to cash, evidently influenced some users of portfolio insurance to implement a strategy via direct stock selling.

Finally, one important feature of portfolio insurance in practice, is that many managers of this strategy usually have to consider the possibility of whether to execute or not execute a transaction, regardless of the indication of their computer program. Because it assumes that volatility remains the same over the period and, in fact, volatility is not stable, there is a possibility that the floor will not be able to be kept.

Index Funds Management

As a result of institutionalisation, institutional investors have increased their use of passive asset management strategies. Index fund managers have used program trading, including orders of basket of stocks, index arbitrage and substitution strategy, and accordingly have used stock index futures contracts. First of all, the most popular way of using stock index futures by index funds is the reinvestment of small cash flows and dividends. Particularly when they are in small amounts, buying underlying stocks is costly in terms of commissions; the index fund is therefore managed temporarily by buying stock index futures until it has enough cash to invest in underlying stocks. Secondly, there is index substitution, which is a kind of index arbitrage by an index fund that aims at profits from arbitrage between stock index futures and underlying stocks. When the futures contract is selling at a sufficient discount to the theoretical value, futures can be substituted for stocks to add additional profits to the index fund, buying cheap futures and selling associated stocks. If the discount abates at or before expiration, the stocks will be repurchased and the futures sold. An index substitution strategy attempts to out-perform the index by index arbitrage. The advantage of index substitution in the US is that since index funds already hold underlying stocks, they can initiate an arbitrage without considering the short sale rules, which require that the short stock must be executed on plus or zero-plus tick.

Thirdly, if there is the possibility of cash outflow, which managers cannot know in advance, managers have to reserve money. In this case, index substitution (buying stock index futures while keeping short-term money) is performed to maintain enough cash. Settlement for stocks sold to get money usually takes a few days, and involves transaction costs. Index substitution therefore offers low costs and convenience in terms of cash flow.

Notes

1. Edwards, Franklin R. (1988) 'Does Futures Trading Increase Stock Market Volatility?', *Financial Analysts Journal*, January-February, 63–69.
2. Goldman Sachs, *World Markets Monthly* (August 1989).
3. The source for much of the descriptive material in this section is to be found in F. J. Fabozzi and G. M. Kipnis (eds) (1989) *The Handbook of Stock Index Futures and Options*, New York, Dow Jones-Irwin.
4. Goldman Sachs, *World Markets Monthly* (August 1989).

Part III
Developments in Accounting and Finance

9 Problems of Assessing Risk and Return Inside an Operating Business

Alan Bainbridge

INTRODUCTION

The process of investment in the UK can be considered as a kind of cash waterfall, whereby capital flows from the investing public via financial intermediaries through the company directors and finally reaching the operational managers who purchase physical assets and human skills in order to create wealth. Legal sanctions, competitive forces and (hopefully enlightened) self-interest act as a pump which forces profits, in the form of cash, back to the shareholders. It is the duty of managers to use shareholders' funds for the purpose of maximising shareholders' wealth.

However, it is a fact of life that operating managers, being more remote, may concern themselves less with the interests of shareholders than do financial intermediaries. This can create substantial problems if shareholder aspirations become seriously at odds with those of managers. The ensuing financial restructuring, mergers, takeovers, leveraged buyouts or closures, although costly, ensure that it is the shareholders who have the last word.

It is therefore in everyone's interest that there should be a full and open dialogue between investors and those entrusted to manage their funds. At the top levels of the investment chain this dialogue is explicit and the Financial Services Act (1986) places a responsibility on financial intermediaries to 'know their customers'. At the operating level, there is also usually an explicit and thoughtful dialogue between managers and bankers and, in owner-managed firms, between shareholders and managers. However, in quoted companies this dialogue is not explicit between managers and shareholders; rather, it is conducted in code, through movements in the share price.

It is perhaps also true that financial intermediaries, and particularly portfolio managers, understand this code better than operating managers. Certainly there is an abundance of academic analysis and theory on the behaviour of share prices aimed at measuring portfolio performance. It is the purpose of this paper to address some of that analysis to the assessment of risk and return on physical assets within operating businesses.

The author is the first to acknowledge that the contents of this paper are not new or original. However, these ideas have not reached the majority of practitioners in *physical* investment appraisal, and the purpose of presenting this paper is to turn up the volume of the message.

THE CAPITAL–ASSET PRICING MODEL (CAPM)

The relationship between risk and return has been extensively studied under the assumptions of efficient markets. The capital–asset pricing model (CAPM) is one of the major results of this work and has been extensively tested using *ex post* data from both UK and US stock exchanges and elsewhere. The attractions of the model are its intellectual pedigree, its relevance to practical situations and its simplicity. It has been extensively described in academic literature (see, e.g., Sharpe, 1964), and is described here only in terms of its conclusions.

The Market Portfolio

Risk is defined in CAPM as the standard deviation of the expected return of an asset. Since an investor is assumed to have a diminishing marginal utility for money, the pain suffered by a shortfall from expectations will be greater than the corresponding pleasure from a windfall gain of a similar amount. Investors are thus risk-averse, and we expect them to demand a higher return from riskier investments.

However, it is a straightforward theory of statistics that a portfolio combining many risky investments will have a lower standard deviation (i.e., risk) than an investment of the same amount in any one of its component securities, provided that the return on the individual investments are not perfectly correlated (i.e., do not move together). This result is intuitively satisfying since we recognise that risks will tend to cancel out if we spread them: 'do not put all your eggs in one basket'. Investors can therefore reduce their risk, without cost, by diversifying, although they cannot remove it entirely.

The corollary is that although investors expect higher returns for higher risk, they do not expect a premium on gratuitous risk which could be removed by diversification.

It can be shown that the most effective portfolio for reducing risk is one which consists of all securities held in proportion to their total capitalisation. This portfolio is called the Market Portfolio and, on the face of it, represents the most efficient distribution of funds in terms of maximising return for risk. Any other portfolio (other things being equal) would increase the risk without a corresponding improvement in return. The risk associated with the Market Portfolio is known as market risk.

This does not mean that investors can chose only one level of risk corresponding to the market portfolio. They may reduce their risk, with corresponding lower average return, by putting some money in the market portfolio and the balance in a risk-free investment such as Treasury bills. Or, they can increase their risk (and average return) by gearing up – that is, by borrowing money and investing it in the market portfolio. These are all efficient portfolios in the sense that their returns will, on average, reflect the level of risk chosen, and there is no gratuitous risk which could be removed by diversification.

The average return on the market portfolio is relatively simple to determine after the event. Clearly it will fluctuate with economic conditions, but has been found to be reasonably stable in both the UK and US, and in both countries stands at a premium of about 9 per cent before personal income tax above the risk-free rate (see 'Risk Management Service', published quarterly by the London Business School).

Of course, other things are not always equal, and some investors may chose to hold portfolios which are different from the market portfolio. Transaction costs, differences in opinion on the interpretation of information, and differing personal circumstances (tax status, for example) may cause some investors to choose personalised portfolios. However, such questions are the concern of the individual or his adviser. They are not known to operating managers of individual firms who perforce must consult the average risk/return requirements represented by the market portfolio.

Market Risk of Individual Securities

It follows from the above considerations that the risk of an individual security has two components. There is a market risk which cannot be

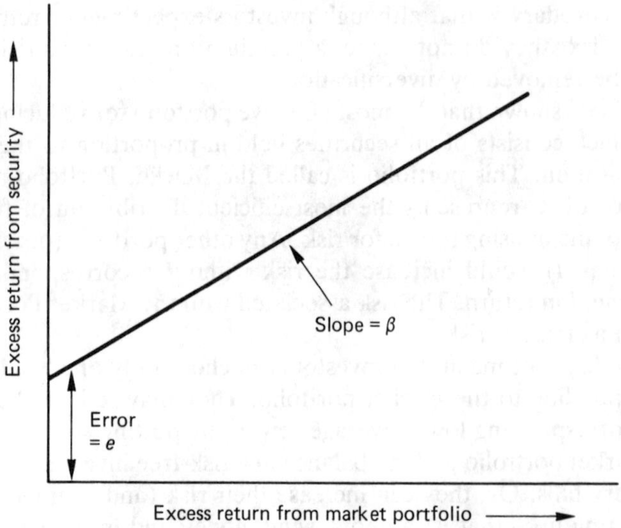

Figure 9.1 Excess return, above-the-risk-free note, of a security compared to the manner portfolio

removed by diversification and which represents the extent to which the return on the security moves in line with (i.e., is correlated to) changes in the overall return from the market portfolio. This is the only type of risk for which investors will require a premium return. Other risks – the specific risks associated with the investment which do not correlate with movements in the market portfolio – can be virtually eliminated in the hands of investors by diversification and therefore they are not expected to produce a premium return.

It is a relatively simple matter to measure the extent to which the return on a security moves in line with the market portfolio simply by plotting it on a graph against the corresponding return from the market portfolio over many periods and drawing a least-squares regression line through the points. The graph is normally plotted in terms of excess returns over and above the prevailing risk-free rate (as shown in Figure 9.1).

The equation of the resulting regression line can be expressed as:

$$\text{Excess return on security} = \beta \times \text{excess return on market portfolio} + \text{Error}$$

Thus the capital–asset pricing model gives a means for measuring the rate of return required from an investment; or, to put it another way more useful to operating managers, the cost of equity capital for the firm.

The equation can be more usefully expressed as follows:

$$R_j = I + \beta M + e \tag{9.1}$$

where R_j is the expected return on the security j
I is the risk-free interest rate (e.g., on Treasury bills)
M is the excess return on the market portfolio above the risk-free interest rate
β is a measure of the correlation between the excess return on the security and the excess return on the market portfolio, and
e is an error which measures the extent to which the security was in fact over- or under-valued compared to the expectations of CAPM, and which for the purpose of the ensuing discussion is assumed to be zero.

THE SIGNIFICANCE OF β AND THE MEASUREMENT OF RISK

Equation (9.1) is the key which breaks the code of the share price mechanism. It provides managers with a means for understanding and determining the risk – and therefore the required rate of return – of their businesses and projects.

β can be determined graphically for any quoted security using the method outlined in the proceeding section. However, it can also be calculated analytically using the following formula derived from regression analysis:

$$\beta = \frac{r_{jm}\sigma_j\sigma_m}{\sigma_m^2} \tag{9.2}$$

where r_{jm} is the expected correlation between possible returns for the security and the market portfolio

σ_j is the standard deviation of the probability distribution of possible returns for security j

σ_m is the standard deviation of the probability distribution of possible returns for the market portfolio

The meaning of β can best be demonstrated using an example. The Risk Management Service of the London Business School publishes quarterly statistics on the variability of all UK quoted securities. In the April 1989 issue shares in Beecham Group plc had a total variability (standard deviation) of 23 per cent, a β of 0.78 and a specific risk (standard deviation) of 16 per cent. The same issue shows that the variability of the all-share index was 22 per cent. This means that the standard deviation of the return on Beecham shares was about 23 per cent of their average return. However, some of this variability is explained by general movements in the UK stock market while some is specific to the Beecham Group itself. The variability explained by the movements in the market is given by:

$$\text{Variability explained by movements in UK stock market} = \beta \times \text{stock market variability}$$

$$= 0.78 \times 22\%$$
$$= 17\%$$

Standard deviations cannot be added linearly, but must be squared first, thus the 23 per cent total variability of Beecham's shares can be analysed as follows:

$$\left(\begin{matrix}\text{Total} \\ \text{variability}\end{matrix}\right)^2 = \left(\begin{matrix}\text{Market-related} \\ \text{variability}\end{matrix}\right)^2 + \left(\begin{matrix}\text{Specific} \\ \text{variability}\end{matrix}\right)^2$$
$$(23\%)^2 \qquad\qquad (17\%)^2 \qquad\qquad (16\%)^2$$

The point, however, is that investors can remove the specific variability almost entirely simply by diversifying their portfolios. For example, the specific variability of the FTSE (100 share) index is only 2 per cent. The market-related variability, however, cannot be removed by diversification and this risk is the only risk which can be expected to attract a premium return. In other words, investors will price Beecham's shares in such a way that the return before income tax is given by R_B where:

$$\begin{aligned} R_B &= \text{I} + \beta M \\ &= 11 + 0.78 \times 9 \\ &= 18\% \end{aligned}$$

(assuming that the risk-free, or Treasury bill, rate is 11 per cent before tax).

The value of β is readily available for all quoted securities and also for stock exchange industry classifications. Historically it has been found that βs are relatively stable over time despite considerable variations in the prices of individual securities. Thus, they provide a simple mechanism whereby managers can assess the required rate of return on investments they make on their shareholders' behalf.

USING β TO ESTABLISH DISCOUNT RATES ON PROJECTS

Armed with the above formulae managers have an intellectual framework, and also a developing analytical tool, for establishing the appropriate discount rate on new projects and the required return on different divisions or businesses within the same enterprise.

The assessment of projects using discounted cash flow (DCF) methods is fairly well developed in UK industry. The accounting and forecasting methods for assessing future cash flows are well documented. However, the discount rates employed in these calculations is often a hit and miss affair; frequently groupwide standard hurdle rates are set, despite the fact that individual subsidiaries may be operating in different industries. At best separate discount rates are established for separate risk classes, but the definition of the risk classes, and the rates assigned to them, often appear arbitrary.

There is a general agreement that higher rates of return are required for higher risk projects but, in the author's experience, the level of understanding of risk is low, and moreover is usually focused on ideas of total risk rather than market risk. The idea of measuring risk is almost completely foreign.

This difficulty in assigning discount rates, coupled possibly with the mathematical complexity of DCF analysis compared to ordinary accounting has, again in the writer's view, compromised the value of this technique in many practical situations. Many major decisions are conceived and evaluated in terms of 'business strategy' rather than 'financial return'. But 'strategy' is an inexact science, and can be a wonderful camouflage for what is nothing more than strongly held beliefs. Financial discipline is essential in assessing economic performance and the viability of proposed investments.

Assessing Cash Flows

The first stage of any project appraisal is an assessment of the project cash flows. This paper is not the place for discussing the various techniques for producing such forecasts, except to point out a common error. In many circumstances, cash flows will depend on the outcomes of specific events; the expected value of such cash flows can be found by producing an average figure using the probabilities of the event outcomes as weights. In following this procedure all that is being calculated is the *expected* value of the cash flow, but some practitioners seem to believe that they are also allowing for risk. This latter belief is not true. The risk is the standard deviation of the expected value and must be assessed separately, and then allowed for in the chosen discount rate.

Choosing a Project β

In choosing a discount rate for a particular project managers must assess the project's risk. However, the risk which should be considered is the extent to which the return on the project is correlated with the stock exchange as a whole (i.e., the market risk of the project). The non-market risk or specific risk of the project is important in measuring the expected return on the project and must be monitored by management to ensure a successful outcome, but *a priori*, for purposes of evaluating an appropriate discount rate, only the market risk need be considered.

The market risk can be expressed in terms of the project's β. In principle this can be calculated using equation (9.2) by estimating the covariance of the project with the market portfolio.

What does this mean?

Effectively it means that managers must assess the extent to which the return on the project is sensitive to economic conditions in the UK as a whole. In the market portfolio, all specific risks have been effectively eliminated, but economywide risks cannot be removed by diversification. For example, the expected return may be sensitive to labour disputes and strikes, but the whole of the British economy is sensitive to such disturbances. The question to be asked is whether the project is more or less sensitive than the average UK investment to such things.

The project β could in principle be calculated directly using equation (9.2). The manager would have to consider a number of different scenarios, estimate their impact on the market portfolio and on the project in question and then calculate the covariance between the two rates of return. However, this is clearly impractical.

A more reasonable approach is simply to use the company's β as the best estimate for the project's β. There are, however, some problems with this approach. One problem is that a company may consist of several different businesses. For example BAT plc, at the time of writing, consists of several businesses including tobacco, insurance and retailing. It may be more appropriate for the retailing business to use an average β value for the retailing industry rather than the β for the BAT company when choosing a discount rate. Fortunately industry βs, by stock exchange classification, are just as easy to obtain as βs for individual securities. Presumably the senior management at BAT monitor the programme of their separate divisions using divisional rates of return appropriate to the divisional risks (i.e., industry βs). If they apply an average company rate of return there is a danger that some divisions will be under-valued while others may be given inappropriate, and perhaps impossible, financial targets.

There are two other issues which require further consideration before determining an appropriate rate of return:

- removing the effects of financial gearing;
- adjusting the company or appropriate industry β for the specific project.

Allowing for Financial Gearing

A further result of CAPM states that investment decisions can, in principle, be made independently of financing decisions (see for example Modigliani and Miller, 1958). Of course, no manager would embark on a project without having the required money available, but the assessment of the financial return on a project can be considered independently of the way in which it will be financed.

In practice, the position may be less straightforward, primarily because of tax considerations. For certain low tax paying companies leasing finance has been highly attractive, although these advantages were significantly reduced when 100 per cent first year tax allowances were removed. More generally, there may be tax advantages for loan finance since interest payments are a tax-allowable cost in the UK. However, it is unclear whether these benefits end up in the hands of borrowers or lenders (who can charge higher marginal interest rates than their clients could otherwise afford).

For the purpose of this paper, we will make the assumption that the method of financing a project has no effect on the project's return. However, financial gearing does affect the variability of shareholders' returns (as opposed to project or asset returns). Generally, the higher a company is geared, the more sensitive is the shareholders' return to fluctuations in the company's performance – that is, the shares have a higher β. The βs measured by monitoring stock exchange returns are equity βs. In assessing a project, we are interested in underlying asset βs, and therefore the equity β must be adjusted for the gearing effect.

Fortunately, this is simple to do. The return on a physical asset is simply a portfolio consisting of equities and loans in proportion to their market gearing. Asset βs can thus be be calculated as the average of equity βs and loan βs using the gearing ratios as weights (ignoring tax effects):

$$\beta_A = \beta_E \times \text{Equity proportion of total finance} + \beta_L \times \text{Loan proportion of total finance}$$

where: β_A is the β of the underlying asset
β_E is the measured β of the company's or industry's equity, and
β_L is the β of the company or industry loans

For most practical situations β_L can be assumed to be zero, but loan βs can be evaluated in precisely the same way as equities if more precise information is required.

Thus as an approximation:

$$\beta_A = \beta_E \times \text{Equity proportion of total finance}$$

Since we are dealing with investments it should be noted that the equity proportion of total finance should *not* be calculated from balance sheet numbers; it is the proportion of the market capitalisation of the company or industry to its market capitalisation plus debt. Clearly this is fairly simple to establish for company βs, but some research may be required to determine industry-wide market gearing factors.

Adjusting Company or Industry βs for the Particular Project

The industry or company β as adjusted for financial gearing may still not represent the best estimate of the project's non-diversifiable risk. Remember that we are trying to assess the correlation between the project's return and the stock market as a whole. So far, we have used the ungeared company (or industry) β as a proxy for this. However, our estimate would be improved if we could also estimate the extent to which the project's return correlated with the company's return. Two factors are particularly important in this regard:

- the operational gearing of the project compared to that of the company (or industry);
- the extent to which the revenues of the project are sensitive to general economic conditions affecting the company or industry.

Operational Gearing and Project Risk

Financial gearing affects the sensitivity of a company's equity return because it is a fixed cost. Generally, if a company or project has relatively high operational fixed costs its return will also be more sensitive to changes in revenue. This risk is not diversifiable; it depends directly on general economic conditions.

Of course, the company's β will reflect the risks inherent in its cost structure. However, a project's cost structure may be significantly different. To see how operational gearing effects risk we have to consider the different elements of cash flow.

$$\text{Net cash flow } (c) = \text{Revenue } (r)\text{-Variable cost } (v)\text{-Fixed cost } (f)$$

Revenue (r) represents all incomes from a company or project. Variable costs (v) are costs which closely correlate with those revenues (e.g., material costs) and fixed costs (f) are other costs (e.g., the initial investment and advertising costs) which do not vary directly with revenues but typically are more a matter of management discretion. Tax charges and allowances will be associated with each category of revenue and cost. The classification of costs as fixed or variable may require care and judgement. For example, it is not always clear that labour is a variable cost, particularly if it is more associated with a machine rather than the volume of output and if there are high redundancy payments associated with reducing manning.

The above expression can be rearranged and discounted to give the following:

$$R = C + V + F$$

where R is the present value of revenue
C is the present value of the net cash flows
V is the present value of variable costs
and F is the present value of fixed costs

Now each of the above terms will correlate with the stock market to a greater or less extent, and we can associate β coefficients with each of them.

The CAPM suggests that the value of the β coefficient of the left-hand term must be equal to the value of the weighted average of the βs of the right-hand side of the equation.

$$\beta_R = \beta_c \frac{C}{R} + \beta_v \frac{V}{R} + \beta_F \frac{F}{R}$$

If we assume that $\beta_v = \beta_R$, since variable costs are proportional to revenue, and further assume that $\beta_F = 0$ then:

$$\beta_R = \beta_c \frac{C}{R} + \beta_R \frac{V}{R}$$

Solving for β_c

$$\beta_c = \beta_R \frac{(R–V)}{C}$$

$$\beta_c = \beta_R \frac{(R–V)}{C}$$

Since

$$R - V = C + F$$

then

$$\beta_c = \beta_R \quad \frac{(C+F)}{C}$$

This shows that the value of the company or project β, β_c, is equal to the β of the its after-tax revenues multiplied by the operating gearing factor

$$\frac{(C+F)}{C}$$

Revenue Sensitivity and Project Risk

We can use the above result to help classify projects into risk classes and to assign them specific β values in order to work out a project discount rate. The idea is to compare the projects' risk to a typical asset in the company, or indeed to the company itself.

From the above:

Project β = Project revenue β × Project operating gearing factor

But we can also write:

Company β = Company revenue β × Company operating gearing factor

Thus, defining relative risk as:

$$\text{Relative risk} = \frac{\text{Project } \beta}{\text{Company } \beta}$$

and dividing the above equations:

$$\text{Relative risk} = \frac{\text{Project revenue } \beta}{\text{Company revenue } \beta} \times \frac{\text{Project gearing factor}}{\text{Company gearing factor}}$$

$$= \quad S \quad \times \quad G$$

The above expression defines two new terms:

$$\text{Revenue sensitivity, } S = \frac{\text{Project revenue } \beta}{\text{Company revenue } \beta}$$

and

$$\text{Relative operational gearing, } G = \frac{\text{Project gearing factor}}{\text{Company gearing factor}}$$

Revenue sensitivity is a measure of the sensitivity of the projects' revenues or sales compared to the company as a whole. It is the area where perhaps the most judgement is required. The following examples may clarify the concept:

- Projects aimed at producing savings in company fixed costs such as computer projects, rationalising head offices and so on, are likely to have a very low revenue sensitivity since they are unlikely to be correlated with changes in the company's sales.
- Projects aimed at producing savings in company variable costs such as scrap reduction projects or perhaps labour saving investments in machinery are likely to have a revenue sensitivity of about 1 since the value of the savings will vary in direct proportion to sales volume.
- Projects which are aimed at increasing company sales in existing products may have revenue sensitivities greater than 1 because competitors will fight to retain market share.

Such judgements are reasonable and normally within management's capability. Typically managers do prepare and review sensitivity analyses on company and project forecasts. This methodology requires that the comparison be done explicitly.

Using the revenue sensitivity factor and the relative operating gearing factor a project's rate of return, R_p, can be calculated as follows:

$$R_p = I + [S \times G \times \beta_A \times M]$$

Summary

The above arguments map out a four-stage process for calculating the required rate of return for a project:

- determine the relevant company or industry β using published information;
- 'un-gear' the company or industry β to remove the effect of financial gearing on equity risk;
- adjust the asset β for relative operational gearing (i.e., cost structure effects);
- adjust the asset β for revenue sensitivity.

The required rate of return can then be calculated as follows using symbols already defined in the text:

$$R_p = I + G.S.\beta_A.\mathrm{M}$$

where β_A is the equity proportion of total finance × β_E.

The above calculation will, as always, require a mixture of analytic method and management judgement. The advantages of this approach can be summarised as follows:

- The focus is on measuring market or non-diversifiable risk which is the only type of risk which investors expect to produce a premium return.
- The effects of financial gearing are explicitly removed when assessing the viability of the project.
- Management's attention is drawn towards considering the risks inherent in a project's cost structure (operational gearing).
- The revenue sensitivity of the project is explicitly examined. This ensures consideration of the fundamental strategic and market effects of the project.

CONCLUSION

The capital–asset pricing model provides a sound and structured approach to the assessment of risk and return within operating businesses. It establishes a clear link between the requirements of investors and investment decisions by managers. Moreover, it provides a key whereby movements in share prices can be interpreted by managers. Many operational managers find share price volatility to be inexplicable nonsense which they cannot relate to the 'real' world.

However, company and industry βs are more stable parameters and they provide an anchor upon which sound investment decisions can be based.

References

Modigliani, F., and Miller, M. (1958) 'The Cost of Capital, Corporation Finance, and the Theory of Investment', *American Economic Review* (June).

Sharpe, W. F. (1964) 'Capital Asset Prices: A Theory of Market Equalisation Under Conditions of Risk', *Journal of Finance* (September).

10 Problems of Income Recognition in a Capital Markets Institution

Richard Stevens

INTRODUCTION

The capital markets today pose many problems for accountants. The apparently simple question 'what is profit?' can and does bring many complex answers. The seemingly obvious answer, that profit is the difference between what the asset is bought for and what the asset is sold for, is rarely that easy to compute. This is particularly so at interim reporting dates when the asset has not been sold. Instead, we have a situation where modern-day players in the market place build highly complex products where the cash return can arise over several periods and the profits have to be accounted for at interim reporting dates. Almost without exception all of today's problems concerning income recognition relate to difficulties as to how to deal with reporting dates during the life of a transaction. In so doing they reveal many deficiencies in accounting theory and practice as a tool for economic decision making.

Almost inevitably much of the debate as to how a particular instrument should be accounted for on its own or in the aggregate will inevitably involve a discussion of 'marking to market' – i.e., the practice of recording an instrument at its market price at an interim reporting date. For many people, marking to market is seen as the panacea for all the problems of income recognition in a capital markets institution. This paper will attempt to show that in practice marking to markets is not as easy as it looks in theory, and thus show why the regulatory response has been so slow.

UNDERLYING ACCOUNTING PRINCIPLES

Before addressing some of the issues that underly current methods of income recognition for capital markets products it is necessary briefly to consider some of the fundamental concepts underlying financial reporting.

Traditionally, financial reporting has had as its foundation a stewardship concept. Essentially, under this basis profit is the difference between what an asset was bought for and what an asset was sold for. It is, in its simplest form, pure cash accounting. In today's market place where all complex money deals are priced by a net present value method at some point in their gestation it can have little relevance at interim dates as the cash has not been realised.

That said, it still remains in use in some parts of the world when valuing a portfolio of outstanding foreign exchange deals. In some parts of continental Europe, for example, a variant of the theme is to value all outstanding foreign exchange deals at a balance sheet date but provide in the accounts only for those items which individually or in the aggregate show losses. Clearly, this method of accounting cannot reflect economic performance measurement. It is undoubtedly a very prudent method and as such has much merit in the stewardship concept. Usually such conservative methods are driven by the imperfections in the market caused by taxation. In continental Europe, particularly, taxation treatment very closely follows accounting treatment.

It is also difficult to have regard for a set of financial statements as a measure of economic performance if there are any hidden reserves in the balance sheet, as is still the case in many sets of financial statements for companies operating in this sector. Indeed this will remain permissible to some extent following enactment of the European Community proposed directive on bank accounts which will permit assets to be undervalued by up to 5 per cent.

However, today's accounts are designed to provide not only a record of stewardship but also an indication of economic performance measurement. Historical cost accounting using the accruals basis has attempted to provide this information. Indeed, all of today's reporting to the stock exchange is done on historical cost accounting basis and is seemingly accepted by analysts and users alike as being useful information for the purposes of economic performance measurement of the company in question. In fact this applies as much to banks and capital markets players as it does to industrial corporations.

It is interesting to reflect that the two concerted attempts to depart from such a framework in both the UK and the US namely Current Purchasing Power (CPP) or Current Cost (CC) accounting have never found favour with users or accounts preparers alike. Profit measures of capital markets players under these frameworks, particularly CC accounting, would look very interesting indeed. However, the concept of what is profit for say, a swap trader under Current Cost Accounting (CCA) is outside the scope of this paper. One thing is, however, certain, it would look radically different from that reported under historical cost accounting and probably much lower than the already small net profits earned in today's highly competitive market place.

Inevitably, problems have arisen with the use of the accruals concept within a historical cost framework when it comes to reflecting products whose original pricing was by reference to the discounting of cash flows arising in the future rather than as a result of past cash transactions or future cash flows at the nominal amount. Consequently, the original purity of the underlying historical cost basis has been eroded by bringing in marking to market concepts in a variety of areas. That being said marking to market is only ever used as a means of making an interim assessment of profit. Realised profit in pure cash terms is still the difference between cost of goods and proceeds of sale of goods.

The whole purpose of marking to market is to provide an estimate of the value of an asset or a liability at the valuation date. The difference between current value and previous value being the profit for the period, the argument is essentially a very simple one. Suppose an institution enters into a speculative foreign exchange contract on 31 October to sell sterling forward with a value date of 30 April. At this time no cash changes hands and so there are no complexities to consider such as the cost of carry in funding the position. At 31 December no cash will have changed hands and unless the contract is given a value no profit or loss will be recorded in the institution's financial statements. Indeed, brokerage may well have been paid reflecting a transaction cost which will have been charged to the profit and loss account. Without attributing a value to the contract there will be no record of the economic performance of the institution, or perhaps more cynically if the contract is showing a profit no basis for calculating the dealer's bonus.

MARKING TO MARKET

It is probably true to say that the UK has been one of the more liberal regimes in permitting marking to market in financial reporting. Such marking to market practices have been accepted for years in permitting the revaluation of property and of investments that were held as part of a trading portfolio. Indeed, the Companies Act has made specific reference to such matters since 1948.

However, in financial services companies probably the most widespread departure from pure historical cost accounting has been in the valuation of outstanding foreign exchange positions. Indeed, the same concepts that underly the valuation of swaps, options, futures and other relevant financial services products have been the *raison d'être* for such marking to market financial institutions.

The driving force behind such an approach has been the need to prepare accounts that reflect the results of the underlying economic activity at an interim reporting date. Consequently, it is necessary that techniques employed for accounting for such activity must mirror as closely as possible those that were used in evaluating whether or not to engage in the economic activity. Furthermore, the method of profit recognition should be such that risk and reward for risk are synchronised with one another. Only if these fundamental attributes are adhered to can the true economic performance of those entering into transactions be properly judged. Any differences between the factors embodied in the appraisal of a decision and the subsequent accounting for that decision are effectively variances in the model.

In practice, there are often differences between the accounting and evaluation models. In such circumstances the company often argues that the original evaluation did not fully address all the matters that were pertinent to the decision to enter into the transaction. In such a case, it is necessary to question how the original decision was taken. It may be the case that a risk not considered at the time of entering into the transaction has now come to the surface. In such a case it is probably relevant to allow for it in the accounting model. But undoubtedly it should be fed back into the evaluation model the next time the model is used. Probably the best way of illustrating the concept of consistency in accounting and evaluation models is to consider the way the bespoke options are valued. There are several mathematical models in use for calculating the price of option contracts under given conditions. Such models generally relate option price to the following parameters:

- market conditions (e.g., market liquidity)
- spot rate
- strike price
- time to expiry
- volatility of the rate
- level of interest rates.

When it comes to valuing the option for accounting purposes it is necessary to evaluate certain attributes of the option. In practice, this often becomes clouded by discussions as to the intrinsic value or time value of an option, but in reality the valuation of a bespoke option has to have regard to the above parameters.

In other words, precisely the same attributes have to be built into the evaluation procedure that were put into the original model for determining whether or not the original deal was a worthwhile undertaking. Of course, many of the parameters employed above are highly subjective and it is this subjectivity that usually gives the greatest degree of difficulty in arriving at a valuation.

PRACTICAL DIFFICULTIES IN MARKING TO MARKET

It is therefore necessary to consider the practical difficulties in marking to market having regard to specific instruments. Generally the first question that has to be asked is: is there a market in the instrument? If there is, the valuation is seemingly relatively easy – a market price is readily available for use. Areas of concern may arise if the market is thin and if the eventual cash movements are some way into the future; and considerations as to whether the bid, mid-market or other rates should be used in particular circumstances. Each of these matters is addressed below.

Marking to Market Where a Market Does not Exist

If a market does not exist, a surrogate must be created by those undertaking the valuation. Inevitably, a wide variety of subjective criteria will need to be addressed. It is these issues that usually present the most difficult practical problems. *Prima facie* it is easy to value an instrument where a market exists, you simply take the market price for the instrument. However, behind this seemingly simple state of affairs there are potential pitfalls.

Bid, Offer or Mid

As noted above, the concept underlying the marking to market is to recognise the profit that would be earned if the deal were closed out today. The pure logic is therefore to use the opposite rate, be it bid or offer, to the rate at which the deal was originally dealt. However, this does not result in the somewhat illogical position that immediately on executing a transaction the institution would need to recognise, as a loss, the spread. Consequently, a mid-market price is frequently taken whereby only half of the spread is immediately lost. As the spread is effectively the transaction cost there is a ground for spreading it over the period to which the contract relates on some systematic and rational basis but this is unworkable in practice.

It is probably the case that if a position is particularly large, and as such its disposal would significantly move the market, then a mid-market price is clearly not going to be obtained and even an offer price may be doubtful, so that there are grounds for taking a prudent value below offer. If the institution is a market maker, the appropriate bid offer price should be used. The practical difficulty comes in determining when something is large.

Net or Gross

A question that often arises is whether the cash flows that are inherent in the marking to market should be considered on a net or a gross basis. Cash flows are frequently allocated into bands of days, weeks, months or years, depending on how far into the future they will arise, and only the net cash flow is valued. Clearly, the impact of netting 2 months against 3 months is much more significant than netting 9 years, 8 months against 9 years, 9 months when considered in present value terms. However, it must be the case that any boundaries will inevitably create some degree of artificiality. The wider those boundaries, and the closer they are to the present day, any error will tend to be exacerbated.

While it is, of course, necessary to consider the practicalities of calculations, in today's highly computerised age, it would appear to be sensible to do everything precisely. The concept of banding really goes back to the time when computer systems were not as sophisticated as they are today. The problem is, however, a wider one than just addressing net and gross cash flows. In practice, this is most commonly applied to foreign exchange traders. Yet foreign exchange contracts are only one user of the nostro accounts: why not apply a valuation criteria to all and every future cash flow? This would lead to valuing by marking to market principles more items than is currently the practice today.

Thin Market

It may be the case that if an institution is holding a large long position of an instrument where the market is thin then the price should be discounted further, or conversely with a short position. In any event the yield will be reduced. Whether adjustment to the market price is in fact necessary depends upon the extent to which the market has already discounted the existence of a known large position. In virtually all markets, except for equities, the existence of the large position will probably be unknown and not reflected in the market price at all. If the price is to be reduced further in the case of a long position, the amount of the reduction will be highly subjective. It is probably preferable that some form of objectivity be applied, unless the market is totally unrealistic.

Also, the valuation method must reflect the reasons for entering into a transaction in the first place. It is tempting to think of marking to market in the narrower sense of the cash which could be obtained if a position were to be liquidated or closed out immediately. For some types of activity this is a perfectly valid basis for valuation. For example, in securities trading, bonds are typically purchased with the intention of reselling them prior to their maturity and hence it is appropriate to value such instruments by direct reference to the current state of the market, although whether one should reflect a known short-term market aberration remains open to debate.

Since valuation typically occurs retrospectively, it is usually possible to identify such short-term aberrations at the time of valuation. There is an argument that if an instrument is held throughout the period of such an aberration then the effect of the aberration should be eliminated from the valuation technique. However, others would argue that, particularly where the aberration creates a more favourable environment, that a profit opportunity may have been missed and that this should be reflected in the results of the activity.

For other types of activity, however, marking to market must be viewed in the much wider sense of being a measure of the economic value to an institution of holding an instrument or position. This view of marking to market is much longer-term in nature and attempts to value, at an interim date, the long-term benefits or costs of having taken a position. In such circumstances, liquidity of the market for the particular instrument is far less important.

Longer-dated Transactions

In principle, the buy-back method is intended to give an indication as to what it would cost the institution to close out that transaction at the valuation date, and thereby lock in a reasonably certain profit subject only to credit risk.

To the extent that the instrument is longer dated, the cash will not be received for some time. Is it therefore correct to regard the difference between the buy and sell price receivable in, say, 10 years' time, as being the true economic value of the profit? Since discounted cashflow (DCF) techniques are effectively employed in the pricing of the instrument, should they not also be employed in the valuation thereof? The difficulty is in determining what is long term. In theory, it is probably appropriate that all profits and losses that are created by marking to market should be discounted back to present-day values. However, for so long as a hybrid approach in accounting is adopted between marking to market assets and liabilities and pure historical cost accounting, there will always be some form of arbitrary split.

If items are to be discounted, then the question as to which interest rate should be used in the discounting arises. For reasons explained below, it is probably appropriate that some form of risk-free zero coupon yield curve be constructed in order to arrive at the relevant discount rate. Such an approach of discounting long-term profits and losses probably takes one automatically down the road of valuing gross, rather than net, positions.

MARKING TO MARKET WHERE NO MARKET EXISTS

Historical Developments

Where no market for the instrument exists, it is necessary to create a surrogate. An examination of the way that swap accounting has evolved provides a very good example of how difficult it can be to create a surrogate that is reasonably objective. It also shows how developments in the market force developments in accounting. Originally individual swaps were accounted for as off-balance sheet loans and deposits. Any fee income was recognised straight away, and net interest flows dealt with on an accruals basis. The need for greater flexibility in the swaps market forced a move into warehousing. The requirement to hedge a swap whilst it remained in the warehouse meant that initial gains or losses on the hedge were generated which then needed to be amortised over the life of the swap transaction.

Initially, these hedge gains and losses were amortised on a straight line basis. As the spreads in the swap market grew finer, reinvestment income and funding costs began to play a greater part in the evaluation of swaps, it became necessary to move to a constant effective yield amortisation profile. Nevertheless, even under warehousing swaps activity, a matched package of swaps and hedge gains/losses from which the total income could be calculated and a sensible amortisation profile established could be constructed. Historical cost accounting had become more difficult, but it was still achievable. The practical difficulties and problems in using traditional historical cost methods to account for swaps became much more acute as the market began to move towards a portfolio basis – that is, splitting the book into its constituent cash flows and using techniques such as duration analysis for managing the entire swap book. Cash flows on swaps became much more complex and the link between swaps and loans and deposits became more tenuous. In addition, hedges were no longer linked to individual swaps, or packages of swaps, but to the book as a whole.

These changes presented serious practical problems in accounting for swaps on an accruals basis. Possibly the most acute of these was ensuring that hedge gains or losses were amortised over the correct period. The period of the amortisation is not immediately apparent. In addition, trying to ensure that all fees and other cash flows in the swap were spread, on a constant effective yield basis, over the correct period demanded a significant input from a large number of high calibre accounting staff. In short, whilst accruals accounting was still possible, it was difficult and, for the larger players arranging the more complex deals, prohibitively expensive.

Even where accruals accounting continued to be applied, a major problem still remained. The move on to a portfolio basis meant that the swap dealers began to evaluate profitability much more on a market value basis than previously. As swap portfolios grew, it became increasingly difficult to reconcile results produced on an accruals or historical basis as produced by the accounting systems with those produced by the dealers on a market value basis. Consequently, an important part of the internal control system ceased to operate.

These practical problems led a number of organisations to switch to market value accounting. It is important to recognise that in many organisations this change was a response to the practical difficulties of accruals accounting rather than a conscious decision by senior management that market value accounting was better. Swaps are marked to market by calculating the net present value of the future cash flows and deducting an income deferred to cover the return on credit risk and future operational costs. Changes in the valuation are then recognised as profit immediately. While this may seem a simple statement, each of those three components is subjective and difficult to measure.

Components of Swap Profit

The return on a swap can be analysed into four discrete portions, all of which have to be addressed in marking to market a swap that is part of a trading position:

- An 'originations' fee' earned for putting the deal together. This is in the nature of a corporate finance fee, and should be recognised at the front end line with the effort expended.
- Profits or losses from managing the position created. This is akin to a dealing activity, and hence the results should be recognised in the same way.
- A return on the credit risk to which the bank is exposed in taking on the swap. This risk extends over the life of the swap, and hence the return should be amortised.
- A return for the continuing operational costs of servicing the swap. Again this income should logically be spread over the life of the swap in order to offset these costs.

Thus, whilst it is logical to recognise *ab initio* that part of the profit represented by origination and dealing, the income derived from credit risk and administrative efforts should be recognised over the life of the swap. Given that under the current capital adequacy requirements the need for capital is determined by the extent of the credit risk, provided that the income deferral for credit is realistic, it should ensure an adequate return on capital on a continuing basis.

In essence, the above suggestion is not radically different from the marking to market methodology currently employed by a number of institutions, although more work is needed on the precise method of calculating the income deferral for credit risk and administrative costs. However, a great deal of confusion appears to have arisen over the nature of this income deferral. It does not represent a provision for possible future losses on the portfolio. Rather, it represents the deferral of the income received for incurring the credit risk and, hence, should be greater than any losses envisaged. In effect, it is similar in nature to the 'turn' on a loan. Having deferred this income, it is then necessary to make provisions out of it, on both a specific and general basis, in order to guard against future losses in exactly the same way as the institution makes provisions against a loan portfolio.

A number of organisations which use market value accounting still maintain an accruals accounting system. But since the total amount of profit recognised is still determined by the valuation, it is not necessary for there to be a high degree of precision about the accruals methodology. Indeed, some organisations accrue only the interest flows on the swaps, ignoring all fees and hedging gains/losses. The reason most commonly given for having both an accruals and a market value system at the same time is uncertainty as to whether the accruals information will be needed for anything, such as correspondence with the tax authorities.

The Discount Rate

In order to arrive at a market valuation of the swap book, it is necessary to discount future cash flows to present value. The discount rate used should be the zero coupon swap rate. It is necessary to use a zero coupon based rate, as any other type of rate includes the combined effect arising out of periodic interest rates which could be reinvested. The zero coupon swap rate is constructed through the interrelationship of a risk-free zero coupon rate and a swap spread. In the case of US dollar cash flows, a zero coupon US Treasury rate is usually used. In determining the zero coupon Treasury rate, it is necessary to restrict the choice of bond to those which are 'on the run' (i.e., being actively traded), as any other will give a distorted result. Clearly, on the run bonds on any date will provide rates only for a specific number of maturities. It is therefore necessary to derive rates for other maturities from those available, so as to convert a Treasury yield curve into a zero coupon yield curve. It is then necessary to calculate the swap spread, which is added to the zero coupon treasury rate in order to determine a discount rate for cash inflows, and subtracted from the zero coupon rate to calculate a discount rate for cash outflows.

In practice, much attention will focus on a sensible measure of the swap spread, given that it could fluctuate in market conditions and could give the dealer scope for profit manipulation. A sensible solution is to take an average swap spread over a period of time, say, 25 days. However, this should be subject to review by a committee of senior management who could alter this spread to allow for any known market trends which may be apparent, and ease the effects that have been dampened by the averaging process.

Practical Application of Swap Marking to Market

To compute the market value of a swap, all relevant components should be included:

- Fixed rate leg
- Floating rate leg
- Hedge portfolio
- Repos and reverse repos
- Cash account

- Initial principal exchanges
- Realised hedge gains and losses
- Interest accruals
- Upfront payments/receipts
- Backend payments/receipts
- Premiums/discounts.

The comments below also assume that accruals accounting is maintained for taxation purposes, and that adjustments are made to bring the accounts on to a marking to market basis. The market value of the fixed and floating cash flows is generated by applying DCF techniques to all future cash flows, using the discount rate as derived above. The hedge portfolio is made up of the current market value (having regard to the comments above on marketable instruments) of all tradeable interest rate hedging instruments.

Repos and reverse repos represent the funding of the hedge positions. For example, in an over-borrowed swap, the swap trader could hedge his fixed position with a long Treasury, and then fund that Treasury position in the repo market. The floating interest payments on the repo also act as a hedge of the floating receipts on the swap. As such, repos and reverse repos should be marked to market. However, since these are often overnight positions, a simplifying assumption that they are at par is often made. This will not always be the case, and identifying the funding components in a pool can be difficult in practice.

The cash account reflects actual cash receipts and payments related to the books swap activity.

Initial Principal Exchanges

These create either a borrowing or investment in the particular book, depending on whether the institution is paying or receiving the principal in the currency of the book at the initial exchange. For example, if it were paying dollars and receiving sterling at the initial exchange the dollar book would have a negative cash position, it would have had to borrow dollars, while the sterling book would have a positive cash balance reflecting the receipt of sterling. Since the far-term exchange is reflected in marking to market of the swap, the initial exchange must also be considered in the marking to market of the book.

Realised Hedge Gains and Losses

Such gains/losses from the sale of hedge positions are included in the cash balance and are amortised to income over the life of the swap. Accordingly, the unamortised balance at any date that is included in the marking to market, is that necessary to reinstate the cash account to the full realised hedge gain or loss. The hedge gains and losses offset the corresponding marking to market gains and losses on the swap position. Since the DCF approach examines cash flows and not accruals, it includes the full coupon amount in the marking to market calculation. Therefore, the discounted calculation must be adjusted for any *accrued interest* which may have been recognised in income.

Initial 'Fee' Payments/Receipts

Those that are compensation for off-market interest rates are included in the cash account. Since these payments are received up front they would not be designated as cash flows in the discounting model. By being excluded from the discounting calculation, the resulting marking to market would either be over- or under-stated, reflecting the off-market rates. To adjust for this, the upfront payment/ receipt must be included in the marking to market calculation. The payment/receipt is amortised over the life of the swap. Accordingly, it is the unamortised balance in the cash account that is included in the adjustment calculation.

Far-term 'Fee' Payments/Receipts

These are also generally considered compensation for off-market rates; however, they would not initially create a cash position as they are not received until the end of the swap. Such a payment/receipt is included in the DCF calculation. To the extent that the far-term payments are also taken to income the discounting calculation must be adjusted by the accreted balance.

In currency exchanges, *premiums* are the amount of principal that the institution receives that is in excess of what it pays. Conversely, *discounts* arise when the institution is paying more than it will receive. In both cases, the discount/premium is considered compensation for off-market interest and/or exchange rites. Both the premium and the discount are amortised over the life of the swap and the cumulative amortised balance in the book marking to market similar to backend payments.

Compensation for Credit Risk

If no adjustment is made in the marking to market of the swap book for credit spread then, assuming no changes in rates of interest, marking to market the swap immediately after entering into the transaction will result in a profit that is a net present value of the compensation being earned for entering into a credit risk. Clearly to recognise such an amount as profit *ab initio* would be inappropriate, as the risk of credit loss remains throughout the swap.

Making some adjustment for credit risk is probably one of the most difficult aspects of marking to market a swap. It is probably fair to say that if there are 10 banks in London who are marking to market the swap books, there are at least 15 different ways in which this adjustment is made. Some of the most common methods are as follows:

- general provision
- by reference to a negotiated credit spread, such as may exist between two parties in the same group

- by deriving a credit equivalent of a bond
- by reference to some external regulator capital adequacy requirement.

This is an area that is of considerable difficulty, where there are no clear-cut answers, and one that is being much researched in practice.

MARKING TO MARKET – ALL, PART OR NONE?

Application of the traditional accounting rules causes some interesting anomalies. For example, consider a bank which purchases a floating rate note (FRN) immediately after the interest rate has been reset which yields 9.3 per cent. The bank match funds the FRN up to the next reset date in 6 month's time at 9.2 per cent. The FRN is purchased for $100 and, ignoring factors other than interest rates, it will again be worth $100 at the end of the 6 months because the coupon will reset to the market level of interest rate.

The profit on this deal is known at the outset, say, 10 basis points. Traditional accounting techniques would designate the FRN a trading asset as it is not being held to maturity. Thus the FRN must be revalued periodically. The coupon on the FRN and the interest expense on the funding are accounted for on an accruals basis, thus spreading the 10 basis point profit over the term of the deal.

Consider now the position after 3 months. Suppose market yields on similar FRNs now stand at 8.0 per cent, giving a value for the FRN of $100.28. Applying 'normal accounting', the FRN would be revalued giving a profit of $0.28 per $100 nominal. Note that this profit is in addition to the 10 basis points net interest income which is still being earned. However, this $0.28 profit cannot actually be there in reality. If the FRN is held for another 3 months, the coupon will reset to 8 per cent (assuming no further changes in interest rates) and the bond price will reset to 100. The bond will then be sold or revalued and the $0.28 profit previously booked will be eliminated.

It has been argued that the $0.28 profit could actually be realised if the bond is sold after 3 months. The elimination of the profit in the subsequent 3 months is a direct result of the decision to keep the FRN. However, this ignores the fact that if the FRN is sold after 3 months, the funding will still be in place at 9.2 per cent for another 3 months. The proceeds from the sale of the FRN can be invested only at 8 per cent (given no change in the credit risk or maturity profile of the book) and hence the bank will earn a negative turn of 1.2 per cent for the remaining 3 months which approximates to the same amount of loss as the profit booked on the bond.

Thus, whatever course of action is taken, the revaluation profit recognised after 3 months, reverses in the second 3 months. It therefore appears somewhat anomalous to recognise this profit in the first place. In order to understand why this anomaly arises, it is necessary to analyse precisely why the price of a security fluctuates. The market value of a security can be computed by discounting the cash flows which the security is expected to produce by the rate of return required by the market on the security. It therefore follows that any change in the value of the security must result either from a change in the expected cash flows or from a change in the rate of return required by the market. Whilst the expected cash flows may change for an equity, in the case of a debt security, the cash flows are certain in the absence of any default. Therefore, with first-class credit ratings, changes in debt security prices are typically caused by changes in the rate of return required by the market.

There are a number of factors which may affect the rate of return which the market expects from a given security. However, one important factor is clearly the current yields on similar instruments. As such yields change, so will the price of the security. Indeed, in the above example, given that we held all other factors constant, it was the sole reason for the change in price.

None of the above is particularly revolutionary, as is well known to people familiar with bond markets. However, it is worth noting that by altering the value of a security as general interest rates change, the market is explicitly recognising a change in the economic value of the FRN from $100.26, explicitly recognising that it is more valuable to own an asset yielding 9.3 per cent as interest rates generally fall to 8 per cent. The same argument can equally be applied to the liability side of the balance sheet. As interest rates fall it must be economically disadvantageous to have funding locked in at a high level. Yet, traditionally, such changes have not been recognised. In the above example, there is no recognition of the fact that the bank has locked in funding at 9.2 per cent when, after 3 months, rates are much lower.

In effect, current revaluation procedures tell only half the story. Assets are revalued because changes in economic value are recognised explicitly through the secondary market prices. Yet for corresponding liabilities no revaluation takes place as there are no secondary markets explicitly to recognise the change in economic value, even though such a change is still there. This situation stems from the narrow definition of revaluation in terms of market (or 'resale') values rather than the wider concept of revaluation measuring changes in economic value.

The obvious way to overcome this problem of asymmetry in current revaluation techniques is to revalue the funding liability. This is where the DCF techniques formulated for swap revaluations are of help. The method is to decompose the funding into a series of cash flows and to discount such cash flows at the prevailing market rates. The calculation below shows how such a technique might be applied to the funding liability in the example, assuming that money market rates have fallen to 7.9 per cent (i.e., the 10 basis points spread between the bond and the funding has remained). It can be seen that by revaluing the liability the revaluation profit on the bond is cancelled out by an opposite loss on the liability and the anomaly in the accounting disappears.

Cash outflow at the end of six months (per \$100 of funding) =

$$\$100 + \$100 \left(0.092 \times \frac{180}{360}\right) = \underline{\$104.60}$$

Value at the end of month 3 based on a three-month rate at 7.9% =

$$\frac{\$104.60}{1 + \left(0.079 \times \frac{90}{360}\right)} = \underline{\$102.57}$$

Carrying value of liability – principal \$100.00

– interest

$$\$100 \times 0.092 \times \frac{90}{360} \qquad \underline{2.30}$$

$$\underline{\$102.30}$$

Revaluation loss = \$102.58 – \$102.30 = $\underline{\$0.28}$

VALUATION OF LIABILITIES

The above example is admittedly a simple one which was chosen specifically to demonstrate the anomaly of revaluing assets without revaluing the corresponding liabilities, and the way in which liability revaluation can correct this. In practice, the maturity profile of a securities portfolio will be far more complex with both assets and liabilities of varying unmatched maturities. Generally, the profile of the asset side will be longer than that of the liability side, particularly where there are fixed rate debt securities in the portfolio. However, the general concepts demonstrated by the above example still stand. Current accounting practices revalue the asset side of the operation but do not attempt to look at the liability side where the results are still accounted for on an accruals basis. Where the funding is on an overnight basis this does not cause a significant error: the profit or loss generated by revaluing the liabilities will not be material. However, the longer the average maturity of the funding, the higher the error. Certainly, with an average maturity for the funding 3–6 months and given a large movement in interest rates, the difference between revaluing and not revaluing the liabilities is likely to be reasonably significant.

The concept of revaluing liabilities, has provoked much discussion within the accounting profession and it is worthwhile dealing with two of the common objections:

– Perhaps the most common objection is that it is not possible to trade a liability and that therefore revaluation accounting is not appropriate. This objection is based on the 'resale' concept of revaluation discussed earlier. Once it is accepted that revaluation is a way of measuring changes in the economic value of the transaction this becomes less of a problem. Indeed, what is arguably more important is change in the economic value from one point in time to another, rather than in the absolute economic value itself. This is important as it allows more flexibility in the selection of revaluation techniques. Provided such techniques, when applied consistently, accurately measure changes in economic value, the accuracy of the value itself is less important.

  This allows revaluation of instruments in one market to be undertaken by reference to rates in another, provided that rates in the two markets behave in the same way. For example, in terms of revaluing funding liabilities, it may be possible to revalue borrowings in a currency linked to the US dollar, by reference to US dollar rates. Initially, allowance may have to be made for the absolute differences in the markets, but after this, provided rates in the two markets move in parallel, the US rates may provide a better source for revaluation prices than a more illiquid market in the correct currency.

- Another objection is that revaluation of liabilities is not permitted by the financial accounting rules. This is true in a number of countries, particularly the US. However, these rules, which are devised primarily for external reporting purposes, should not preclude such revaluation taking place for internal purposes where accurate measurement of profit for control and management decision making is much more important.

ACCOUNTING AND LEGAL FORM

So long as parts of the balance sheet are treated differently to other parts a range of accounting issues will arise. The foreign exchange market provides some simple examples. Consider the situation of a dealer who enters into a forward-forward contract. He could equally have purchased a future rate agreement. If he enters into a forward-forward that would probably be accounted for within the foreign exchange valuation. If he had entered into an FRA it would probably have been valued as if it was part of a trading portfolio and income taken to the profit and loss account. Equally, if it had been part of a hedge transaction any gain or loss in the value of the FRA would have been deferred and amortised over the period that the hedge intended to be effective.

However, it could equally be argued that a forward-forward transaction like a spot against forward transaction is merely a funding transaction; no exchange exposure was intented to arise. If the transaction had been linked together with present or future loans and deposits then the difference between the forward exchange rates would have been held up in the balance sheets and amortised over the period of the related deposits and loans.

In other words, one apparently straightforward transaction can be accounted for in different ways according to how it is defined and what the intentions of the parties are. Any effective policing of such a market is therefore very difficult indeed.

Divergent accounting treatments can also arise according to the exact legal form of a transaction. This problem can best be illustrated by two examples related to the swap market. In the first case supposing an institution enters into a foreign exchange contract which is long term in nature. Such a contract will be accounted for on a marking to market basis. Exactly the same economic result could have been achieved by entering into a currency swap. The only difference between the two is that the foreign exchange contract would have been dealt with over the telephone without formal legal agreement. The swap contract would have been dealt with in the same way over the telephone, but evidenced by a formal legal contract. In the case of the swap it is perfectly possible that it would be accounted for on an accruals basis. Thus you may have one organisation entering into economically the same contract through two different sources. What the contract is called will influence its accounting, and thus its reported profit.

The formal definition of a contract is also behind the second example. Suppose a bank takes a fixed-term deposit with a zero rate of interest but an incremental repayment of principal to reflect the absence of a coupon during the term of the deposit. A similar transaction could have been structured as a zero coupon swap agreement. Again the difference is in the legal form of the transaction. In the former it is necessary for the institution to be authorised under the Banking Act in order to engage in the activity. In the latter no such authorisation is required. In accounting terms, in the bank taking the zero coupon deposit it is almost definitely the case that the deposit will not be valued at market to reflect changes in interest rates. In the case of the zero coupon swap it is probable that economically the same transaction will be valued in the accounts on a marking to market principle. Once again, the legal form can result in different accounting treatments for what is in practice the same transaction.

A further anomaly can come out of the swap market. Frequently a swap is written on the back of a large Eurobond transaction. Developments in the market place are such that today the swap can also be as part of a repackaging of existing bond issues. Suppose the institution is entering into a repackaging of existing holdings of Eurobonds, probably for a third party. Let us also assume that the institution accounts for its bonds on a market value basis and accounts for its swaps on an accruals basis. In the overall repackaging the customer will be quoted only one price. However, that price will be partly to do with the price of the bonds and partly to do with the price of the swap. If for accounting purposes part are dealt with on a market value basis and part are dealt with on an accruals basis, it becomes necessary to find some method of allocating the overall yield on the transaction to the two components. In practice, this would be done by reference to some surrogate external market which attempts to decompose the transaction into its integral components. But the amount of management time this takes is inordinate and very wasteful.

So have we not built an accounting basis which is inappropriate? The somewhat unconventional mix of historical cost and market value accounting has brought about the position where the accounts may have a questionable value as a mechanism of reflecting economic performance in a period. Pure historical cost accounting doesn't achieve this, yet the halfway house of valuing assets and not valuing liabilities is equally dangerous.

REGULATORY RESPONSE

The regulators themselves have not managed to respond to the challenge. In the UK the provisions of the EC Fourth Directive on Company Accounts as embodied in the Companies Act 1981 apply to non-bank financial institutions but don't address these issues. As far as banks are concerned their accounts are still dealt with under the old provisions of the Companies Act 1948. The EC Bank Accounts Directive will also be equally powerless.

As far as self-regulation is concerned in the UK the Accounting Standards Committee (ASC) has not even begun to attempt to address such complicated issues. If one turns to the United States, the Financial Accounting Standards Board (FASB) has a project which is expected to develop broad standards aimed at resolving issues raised by the inconsistent practice and guidance that have developed for new financial institutions and transactions over the years. In so doing the Board is considering the financial instrument recognition and measurement issues using a fundamental financial instrument approach. This approach is base on the premise that all financial instruments are made up from a few building blocks (i.e., the fundamental financial instruments), and that resolving the accounting issues related to those building block instruments will help resolve the accounting issues related to the other instruments.

The FASB's deliberations are expected to lead to the preparation of a discussion document that will include some preliminary conclusions. It is unlikely that the discussion document will be issued before 1990. There will then be a need to have an exposure draft before a standard is published, so a long period must be expected here. Undoubtedly it will be the case that if the FASB does produce some workable proposals they will tend to be followed by many players around the world irrespective of the jurisdiction under which they report.

Other US regulatory bodies have attempted to become involved. The Securities Exchange Commission (SEC) has traditionally attempted to deal only with disclosure rather than income recognition matters. However, in late 1989 the staff of the SEC indicated that it may look to the regulatory accounting standards in assessing the generally accepted accounting principals for swaps. A proposed regulatory standard was put forward at the same time by the Federal Financial Institutions Examination Council (FFIEC), which is effectively part of the Federal Reserve Board. This paper essentially proposed that swap profit be recognised by marking to market the swap at inception and spreading the gain over the life of the swap. Not surprisingly this met with virtually universal hostility amongst the major swap players, particularly those who were marking to market in their financial statements. Despite a very short exposure period for the FFIEC proposals, little or nothing has been heard of them since the start of 1989.

What it did, however, introduce was a concern amongst the major players in the market that a potential difference was developing between Regulatory Accounting Principals (RAP) applied in filings of bank regulators and Generally Accepted Accounting Principles (GAAP) required to be used for general purpose external financial reporting. Not surprisingly, the swap players argue that so called RAP – GAAP differences are costly to the preparers of financial information and potentially confusing to users of that information. There will, however, always be the conflict between the regulator who likes to have a system of accounting or financial measurement that is relatively objective compared to a preparer of such information who would like to leave it as subjective as possible. However, it is inherently costly to maintain transaction records based on two different methods of accounting and provided that a basis of GAAP can be arrived at which properly measures economic performance there should not be a need for the regulator to define his own method of accounting.

Accordingly it can be seen that there is a long way to go in accounting for any of the modern capital markets products. The FASB project offers by far the greatest possibilities, and the two fundamental objectives underlying it are that:

1. similar financial instruments should receive similar accounting treatment;
1. accounting for financial instruments should be consistently applied from company to company.

Many of the difficult and perplexing accounting issues today rise from the patchwork of standards issued over time dealing with a variety of individual types of instruments. Currently there are separate standards addressing foreign currency transactions, future contracts, collaterised mortgage obligations, receivable sales, long-term debt, zero coupon instruments, options, sales of securities with puts, and many others issued by the FASB, its emerging issues taskforce or other bodies.

The fact that the FASB is going back to first principles to determine how such complex economic instruments should be presented has to be welcomed. One thing, however, is clear: some of the fundamental conflicts in accounting are going to emerge again. Pure historical cost accounting, while providing a good measure of stewardship will not provide any measure of economic performance. A system that is based on a halfway house of pure historical cost accounting and market value accounting is potentially misleading in that it neither achieves a stewardship objective nor a proper measure of economic performance. To apply fully a market value-based accounting system might contain so many practical subjectivities that its value for economic performance measurement or stewardship would be questioned. If the latter route is adopted it will certainly place the auditor in some difficult positions in acting with the wisdom of Solomon as to whether the market values that are applied to individual transactions are reasonable.

Index